Barbarossa

By the Editors of Time-Life Books

Alexandria, Virginia

TIME
LIFE ®

Time-Life Books is a division of
Time Life Inc., a wholly owned subsidiary of

The Time Inc. Book Company
Time-Life Books

Managing Editor: Thomas H. Flaherty
Director of Editorial Resources:
Elise D. Ritter-Clough
Director of Photography and Research:
John Conrad Weiser
Editorial Board: Dale M. Brown, Roberta Conlan,
Laura Foreman, Lee Hassig, Jim Hicks, Blaine
Marshall, Rita Thievon Mullin, Henry Woodhead

PUBLISHER: Joseph J. Ward

Associate Publisher: Ann Mirabito
Editorial Director: Russ Adams
Marketing Director: Anne Everhart
Director of Design: Louis Klein
Production Manager: Prue Harris
Supervisor of Quality Control: James King

The Third Reich

SERIES DIRECTOR: Thomas H. Flaherty
Series Administrators: Jane Edwin,
Jane A. Martin
Editorial Staff for *Barbarossa:*
Designer: Raymond Ripper
Picture Editor: Jane Coughran
Text Editors: Stephen G. Hyslop, John Newton,
Henry Woodhead
Researcher: Maggie Debelius
Assistant Designer: Lorraine D. Rivard
Copy Coordinator: Charles J. Hagner
Picture Coordinator: Jennifer A. Iker
Editorial Assistant: Jayne A. L. Dover

Special Contributors: Ronald H. Bailey,
Lydia Preston Hicks, Brian C. Pohanka, David S.
Thomson (text); Martha-Lee Beckington,
Ann-Louise Gates, Oobie Gleysteen (research);
Michael Kalen Smith (index)

Editorial Operations
Production: Celia Beattie
Library: Louise D. Forstall

Computer Composition: Gordon E. Buck
(Manager), Deborah G. Tait, Monika D. Thayer,
Janet Barnes Syring, Lillian Daniels

Correspondents: Elisabeth Kraemer-Singh
(Bonn), Christina Lieberman (New York), Maria
Vincenza Aloisi (Paris), Ann Natanson (Rome).
Valuable assistance was also provided by: Judy
Aspinall, Elizabeth Brown (New York); Barbara
Hicks, Christine Hinze (London); Sasha
Isachenko, Felix Rosenthal (Moscow).

Other Publications:

TIME-LIFE LIBRARY OF CURIOUS AND UNUSUAL FACTS
AMERICAN COUNTRY
VOYAGE THROUGH THE UNIVERSE
THE TIME-LIFE GARDENER'S GUIDE
MYSTERIES OF THE UNKNOWN
TIME FRAME
FIX IT YOURSELF
FITNESS, HEALTH & NUTRITION
SUCCESSFUL PARENTING
HEALTHY HOME COOKING
UNDERSTANDING COMPUTERS
LIBRARY OF NATIONS
THE ENCHANTED WORLD
THE KODAK LIBRARY OF CREATIVE PHOTOGRAPHY
GREAT MEALS IN MINUTES
THE CIVIL WAR
PLANET EARTH
COLLECTOR'S LIBRARY OF THE CIVIL WAR
THE EPIC OF FLIGHT
THE GOOD COOK
WORLD WAR II
HOME REPAIR AND IMPROVEMENT
THE OLD WEST

For information on and a full description of any
of the Time-Life Books series listed above, please
call 1-800-621-7026 or write:
Reader Information
Time-Life Customer Service
P.O. Box C-32068
Richmond, Virginia 23261-2068

The Cover: Flattened against the snow, German
infantrymen supported by a Panzer III, one of a
dwindling number of tanks still running in late
1941, return Soviet fire west of Moscow. The Wehrmacht, after completing the greatest sustained offensive in military history, was stopped by the Russian winter and the Red Army, frustrating Adolf
Hitler's grand scheme to conquer the Soviet Union
in a single "lightning campaign."

This volume is one of a series that chronicles
the rise and eventual fall of Nazi Germany. Other
books in the series include:
The SS
Fists of Steel
Storming to Power
The New Order
The Reach for Empire
Lightning War
Wolf Packs
Conquest of the Balkans
Afrikakorps
The Center of the Web
War on the High Seas
The Twisted Dream

Second printing. Revised 1991. Printed in U.S.A.

Published simultaneously in Canada.
School and library distribution by Silver Burdett
Company, Morristown, New Jersey 07960.

TIME-LIFE is a trademark of Time Warner Inc.
U.S.A.

**Library of Congress Cataloging in
Publication Data**
Barbarossa / by the editors of Time-Life Books.
    p.   cm. — (The Third Reich)
Includes bibliographical references.
ISBN 0-8094-6991-X.
ISBN 0-8094-6992-8 (lib. bdg.)
    1. World War, 1939-1945—Campaigns—
Eastern. I. Time-Life Books. II. Series.
D764.B219 1990   940.54'21—dc20   90-10781

General Consultants

Col. John R. Elting, USA (Ret.), former asso-
ciate professor at West Point, has written or
edited some twenty books, including *Swords
around a Throne, The Superstrategists,* and
American Army Life, as well as *Battles for
Scandinavia* in the Time-Life Books World
War II series. He was chief consultant to the
Time-Life series, The Civil War.

Charles V. P. von Luttichau is an associate at
the U.S. Army Center of Military History in
Washington, D.C., and coauthor of *Command Decision* and *Great Battles.* From 1937
to 1945, he served in the German air force
and taught at the Air Force Academy in Berlin. After the war, he emigrated to the United
States and was a historian in the Office of the
Chief of Military History, Department of the
Army, from 1951 to 1986, when he retired.

Williamson Murray is a professor of European military history at Ohio State University
and has been a visiting professor at the Naval
War College. He has written numerous articles and books on military affairs, including
The Luftwaffe, 1933-1944, and *The Change in
the European Balance of Power, 1938-1939.*
He has also coedited the three-volume
study, *Military Effectiveness.*

Contents

Entering a Land without End

"At the beginning of each campaign," Adolf Hitler confided to an aide before his momentous invasion of the Soviet Union, "one pushes a door into a dark, unseen room. One can never know what is hiding inside."

Indeed, the German armies that so confidently crossed the Russian frontier on June 22, 1941, found themselves in an alien land of stupefying magnitudes. The vast forests of the north were as impenetrable as jungle. Swamps larger than entire German provinces blocked the advance. In the south, the undulating plains of the Ukraine swept unbroken from horizon to horizon. Boundless Russia seemed able to swallow the German armies whole. "There was no limit to it," one soldier

Rolling into Russia in the summer of 1941, German panzers pass Soviet tanks knocked out early in the campaign.

Albrecht Schimpf, would recall. "We could see no end."

There was no end, either, to the defenders' resilience. Despite losing half a million men killed or wounded in the first two weeks, the Soviets kept coming from an apparently bottomless reserve. A Wehrmacht colonel likened the German army to an elephant attacking ants: "The elephant will kill thousands, maybe millions, but in the end, the ants' numbers will overcome him, and he will be eaten to the bone."

The climate, too, conspired against the invaders. Autumn rains turned primitive roads to a deep muck that gripped wheeled vehicles like glue and sucked the boots from the feet of German infantrymen. Then the temperature dropped, the first snows fell, and "General Winter," as the soldiers called it, arrived to claim the battlefield. The Wehrmacht's machines of war froze. Within sight of Moscow, the German army stalled, and the nightmare of a winter in the Soviet Union began

German infantrymen paddle inflatable rafts across a river in the forbidding Pripet Marshes of western Russia.

On the road to Minsk, German antitank gunners duel with the Soviets as smoke billows from a stricken armored car.

A German motorcyclist contemplates Kharkov's spacious Red Square. The city fell to the Wehrmacht on October 24, 1941.

A column of Soviet prisoners of war winds through a snow-clad Russian hamlet toward internment in the German rear.

German soldiers in commandeered peasant carts called *Panjes* slog over a muddy track impassable to motorized traffic.

ONE

"The World Will Hold Its Breath"

Although it was the shortest night of the year, the wait until dawn on Sunday, June 22, 1941, seemed endless to the German troops massed on the frontier of the Soviet Union. The previous evening, Adolf Hitler had addressed them for the first time as "soldiers of the eastern front" in an order of the day that defined their mission. They were about to invade the world's largest nation. Along a border that twisted and turned for 1,350 miles between the Baltic and the Black Sea, they huddled expectantly in forests, grainfields, and pastures. Soon, with the first hint of light in the eastern sky, the flash and thunder of their heavy artillery would announce Operation Barbarossa, Hitler's grand bid to subdue the land that had defied even Napoléon Bonaparte.

"The world will hold its breath," Hitler said, without exaggeration. Never before had a nation assembled such an enormous force to launch a military operation. More than three million men were deployed on Russia's western border; with them were 3,300 tanks, 600,000 other vehicles, more than 7,000 artillery pieces, 2,770 airplanes, and 625,000 horses. This was the mighty Wehrmacht, which in less than two years had triumphed in whirlwind campaigns against Poland, Norway, Denmark, the Netherlands, Belgium, Luxembourg, France, Yugoslavia, and Greece.

The magnitude of the latest task, however, was beyond precedent. The Soviet Union sprawled over one-sixth of the earth's land mass, supported a population of about 200 million people—more than twice that of Germany—and featured severe extremes of temperature and terrain. Nevertheless, Hitler and most of the army high command anticipated a short campaign. They believed Operation Barbarossa would last no longer than ten weeks. So certain were they of swift summer success that the planners had ordered winter clothing for only one-third of the invasion force.

The rank and file, buoyed by their string of victories, had good reason to share their leaders' confidence. As the minutes ticked away before the beginning of the largest and bloodiest campaign in modern military history, groups of sleepless men toasted the success of this new war with

A column of German infantry trudges down a Russian road on a summer day in 1941. The dust and heat soon gave way to mud and cold. "Climate in Russia," a German general grumbled, "is a series of natural disasters."

special rations of brandy and with vintage Champagne they had lugged from France. The soldiers did not dwell on the fact that 129 years earlier, nearly to the day, Napoléon's doomed legions had crossed the Niemen River en route to Moscow.

Hitler's decision to invade Russia grew directly from three driving concerns of national socialism: race, space, and anticommunism. Hitler and his party had unconcealed contempt for the Slavs. He lumped them with the Jews as an inferior race and equated bolshevism with Zionism. The Slavs, he said, were "vermin" and "subhumans" who were intended to serve the Aryan master race. Race and ideology, however, were only part of Hitler's philosophy. From the earliest days of nazism, Hitler had looked eastward to find lebensraum, or living space, for the German people. "If we speak of new land in Europe today, we can primarily have in mind only Russia and her vassal border states," he wrote in *Mein Kampf.* "Here fate itself seems desirous of giving us a sign."

Hitler's sense of destiny in the east dictated his overall strategy for war. His strike into Poland on September 1, 1939, had been the first major step eastward. In order to ensure its success, he had signed a nonaggression pact with the Soviets, who were given the franchise to gobble up eastern Poland and the Baltic states after Germany conquered western Poland. This guarantee of peace on the eastern front served Hitler's interests by protecting Germany's rear while the Wehrmacht invaded Scandinavia, the Low Countries, and France. Then, once his western flank was secure, his plan was to turn eastward again. The agreement with the Russians "was meant only to stall for time," Hitler smugly told members of his inner circle. "We will crush the Soviet Union."

On July 21, 1940, scarcely a month after the conquest of France, Hitler instructed his military leaders to prepare for an invasion of the Soviet Union, to be launched no later than the following spring. He cited two reasons for wanting to attack Russia. One was the danger that the Russians themselves would initiate a war against Germany. While the Germans were preoccupied in western Europe, the Soviet dictator, Josef Stalin, had acted aggressively. During June of 1940, he had occupied the three Baltic nations of Estonia, Latvia, and Lithuania and the eastern Rumanian province of Bessarabia, all of which Hitler had granted to the Russian sphere of influence under the nonaggression pact. Then Stalin greedily grabbed for more. He seized a strip of western Lithuania reserved for Germany under the treaty and marched into the Rumanian province of Northern Bukovina, which had not been part of the deal. Stalin had also attacked Finland, a friend and chief source of nickel for the Reich.

The face of a Soviet prisoner of war, labeled an *Untermensch*, or subhuman, appears on the cover of an SS pamphlet intended to convince German soldiers that their Slavic enemies were racially inferior. The Soviets, declared a Nazi tract, had been "rendered stupid, provided with blinkers, proletarianized, and made into machines."

Hitler's other stated reason for the invasion of Russia related to Great Britain. The British had been driven from the Continent but had not been vanquished, although the Luftwaffe planned an aerial blitz against the island nation that August and Hitler projected an actual invasion, Operation Sea Lion, to follow. Hitler contended that the British were holding out in hope of Russian intervention. "Russia," he said, "is England's continental sword." Once the Russians were defeated, the German leader argued, the British, too, would succumb.

In fact, it was the prospect of fighting a two-front war as in World War I—against the Russians and the British simultaneously—that caused a handful of dissidents in the German high command to speak out against the invasion of the Soviet Union. Their arguments failed to sway Hitler. The Führer had decided, irrevocably, to "settle accounts with Russia as soon as fair weather permitted."

Planning for the Russian offensive, inherently difficult because of the venture's scope, was further complicated by the German military's overlapping command structure. In 1938, when Hitler fired his leading generals and took over as commander in chief of the armed forces, he had created his own military staff. Known as the OKW—*Oberkommando der Wehrmacht*, or armed forces high command—it immediately crossed swords with the OKH—*Oberkommando des Heeres*, or army high command.

During the latter half of 1940, both staffs developed plans for the attack on Russia. To be sure, the plans shared many features. Both called for rapid armored strikes similar to the blitzkrieg that had proved successful against Poland and France. These thrusts would aim to encircle huge segments of the Soviet armies in western Russia before the troops could retreat to the relative safety of the hinterland.

The Germans also envisioned conquering only the western quarter of Russia. Ultimately, the Wehrmacht would come to a halt roughly 1,200 miles beyond the border, along a line that would run south from Archangel, on the White Sea, to Astrakhan, on the Caspian Sea. Beyond this objective

On a 1940 visit to Berlin, the Soviet foreign minister, Vyacheslav Molotov (*far left*), confers through an interpreter with the Nazi interior minister, Wilhelm Frick, while, at right, Foreign Minister Joachim von Ribbentrop and SS chief Heinrich Himmler enjoy cigars. The meeting failed to relieve strained relations between the Soviet Union and the Reich.

line lay a vast expanse of Asia that the Germans regarded as an unproductive wasteland, not worth occupying.

The two staffs—OKW and OKH—split sharply in their views of the campaign's strategic objectives. These differences were personalized in a dispute between Hitler and the chief of the army high command, General Franz Halder. Hitler preferred a three-pronged attack of the type submitted by his OKW staff: A northern army group would strike through the Baltic states toward Leningrad; a southern group would push through the Ukraine to Kiev and beyond; and a central group would slice through Belorussia, the Soviet republic that lay astride the route to Moscow.

Hitler, for a combination of reasons, was attracted by the opportunities on the two flanks. The northern attack would secure the vital ports on the Baltic Sea and eliminate the city of Leningrad, an important economic center that Hitler detested as the philosophical cradle of bolshevism. The southern thrust could lead to the occupation of the Soviet breadbasket in the Ukraine and beyond it, the coal-rich, industrialized Donets Basin. Of course, successful flank attacks would also provide protection for the advance on the Soviet capital.

The capture of Moscow itself, Hitler told his generals, "was not so very important." After all, he pointed out, it was at Moscow that Napoléon's campaign had foundered in 1812: "Only completely ossified brains, absorbed in the ideas of past centuries," said Hitler, "could see any worthwhile objective in taking the capital."

Although Hitler relegated Moscow to secondary importance, General Halder made it the centerpiece of the strategy he advocated. The fifty-six-year-old Halder was a product of the old-line Prussian general staff, and he guarded the army's prerogatives with cunning and icy logic, even if it meant arguing with the Führer. Owlish and professorial in appearance and manner—Hitler once referred to him as a "chronic know-it-all"—he commissioned at least three studies of invasion possibilities. From these, he concluded that Moscow must remain the primary objective of Germany's invasion of the Soviet Union.

Both Halder and his superior, Field Marshal Walther von Brauchitsch, the army commander in chief, contended that the capture of Moscow would deprive the Soviets not only of their seat of government but also of a major armaments center and communications hub. In their view, merely the threat of the loss of the capital would compel the Red Army to concentrate its forces to defend the city, giving the invaders an opportunity to surround and destroy them.

The final plan for the invasion was contained in Hitler's top-secret Directive 21. The supreme commander gave the operation a name with

historical significance to replace its former nondescript working titles, "Otto" and "Fritz." He called it Barbarossa—Red Beard—after the nickname of Frederick I, the twelfth-century emperor who successfully made war on the Slavs and died on a Crusade to the Holy Land.

The Barbarossa directive called for three army groups to push toward Leningrad, Moscow, and Kiev *(map, page 27)*. Moscow, however, would remain a secondary objective. When the center group reached the area just east of Smolensk, about two-thirds of the way between the border and Moscow, it would divert its armor northward to help clear the Baltic region and southward to help secure the Ukraine. In the words of the directive, "Only after the fulfillment of this first essential task, which must include the occupation of Leningrad and Kronstadt, will the attack be continued with the intention of occupying Moscow." That settled the matter in Hitler's mind, but not in Halder's. The disagreement between him and Hitler—and their OKH and OKW staffs—would initiate additional fighting over strategic objectives, with fateful consequences for the Wehrmacht.

Even as the Barbarossa directive was drafted, map exercises and other war games conducted by Major General Friedrich von Paulus, deputy chief of the army high command, revealed potential problems awaiting the ambitious enterprise. The Wehrmacht was accustomed to operating within the comparatively limited confines of central and western Europe. In Russia, it would have to cover enormous distances. The German front in Russia would have to expand funnel-like from the western frontier to well over 2,000 miles wide as the invaders progressed. Paulus's studies showed that even an army of more than three million would be spread desperately thin soon after the invasion.

The army would have to pace its blitzkrieg tactics differently in a country so vast. The armored spearheads would quickly outrun the infantry, leaving large and vulnerable gaps in between. As the spearheads penetrated ever deeper into the heartland, resupply would become critical. Russia had few substantial highways: Only three percent of the roads in the European part of the country were paved. The few east-west railroads were mostly single lines and consisted of broad-gauge tracks incompatible with German and central European trains.

German planning presupposed a decisive superiority over the Russians in the quality of fighting men and in equipment, leadership, and tactics. In sheer number of soldiers, the two sides would be approximately equal. The German army would deploy 3.3 million men—about 87 percent of its 3.8 million total; the Red Army consisted of about 3.4 million ground troops. The Germans knew that the enemy possessed huge quantities of war machines. German intelligence showed the Soviets could muster 12,000 planes and 22,700 tanks against the 2,770 German aircraft and 3,300 panzers that would be deployed in Russia. The great bulk of these Soviet machines, however, were outmoded and useless for modern warfare. Most of the airplanes lacked radios, and pilots had to resort to wing wagging in order to send signals. And the Red Army still maintained more than a dozen divisions of horse cavalry.

The Germans also knew that the Soviets lacked experienced leaders. Stalin's political purges, which had begun in 1937, destroyed the officer corps. An estimated 30,000 army and navy officers were executed, including 90 percent of the generals and 80 percent of the colonels. The result became painfully clear during the Soviet invasion of Finland in 1939, when more

Flanked by Walther von Brauchitsch (left), the army's commander in chief, and Franz Halder, the chief of the army high command, Hitler charts the invasion of Russia. The generals wanted to concentrate their forces in a drive on Moscow, but Hitler overruled them.

than one million ineptly led Russians were required to subdue a Finnish army that numbered barely 200,000. The Finnish commander in chief likened the Soviet performance to that of a badly conducted orchestra whose players could not keep time.

These obvious Russian shortcomings led Hitler and his planners to underestimate their enemy's military potential. Reich intelligence operatives had failed to penetrate the rigid Soviet state; they had been unable to produce adequate topographic maps, let alone accurate projections of future weapons production. Unknown to the Germans, new industrial cities were springing up in the Ural Mountains and farther east in Soviet Asia. And the Red Army could recruit from practically limitless reservoirs of manpower: 17 million Soviet males were of prime military age.

At the same time, the Germans overestimated their own strength. The euphoria arising from recent victories caused them to overlook the flaws in their military machine. The army still depended mainly on infantry that traveled on foot and relied heavily on horses to move its artillery and supplies. Even the motorized infantry divisions, which had proved vital to the success of the armored spearheads, were short of trucks, despite having pressed into service thousands of commercial vehicles commandeered in Germany or captured in France.

The panzer divisions themselves possessed less striking power than it appeared. Since crushing France, Hitler had doubled the number of tank divisions, from ten to twenty, largely through the stratagem of cutting in half the number of tanks assigned to each division. This reduced the number per division to about 160. Tank divisions were now a fairly potent mix of Panzer IIIs, Panzer IVs, and lighter Czech tanks; most of the smaller, lightly armed Panzer Is and IIs were limited to reconnaissance duty or were cannibalized for their chassis. The next generation of panzer was still in the prototype stage or on the

Three Revolutionary heroes, Semyon Budenny (*left*)**, Semyon Timoshenko** (*standing*)**, and Kliment Voroshilov, shown in 1919, survived Stalin's purges to emerge as heroes again in 1941.**

Artillery tractors tow 152-mm howitzers through Red Square in Moscow on November 7, 1940, to observe the twenty-third anniversary of the Bolshevik Revolution. These guns, like much Soviet weaponry, had been introduced in the 1930s.

drawing boards of German engineers. The Soviets, in fact, were ahead of the Germans in tank development. During the spring of 1941, when Hitler was still feigning friendship, he allowed a Russian military commission to visit his tank factories. The Soviet officers, who knew that their assembly lines at home were beginning to turn out faster and heavier tanks, refused to believe that the Panzer IV was Germany's heaviest tank.

Germany's armor situation posed a paradox. The Wehrmacht lacked tanks and trucks because Germany's industry had not yet geared up for all-out war. This failure to fully mobilize the economy rendered all the more vital the compelling concept of blitzkrieg, which promised quick victory through lightning-fast strikes. And yet blitzkrieg depended on mobility, which in turn required the increased production and improvement of trucks, tanks, and other vehicles.

In any event, Hitler and many of his generals were convinced of their invincibility—and of the Soviets' inferiority. They were so confident of rapid victory that they made no serious attempt to enlist the aid of their Axis partner Japan, which for years had been at odds with the Soviet Union. Although an attack from the east would have diverted Soviet energies, Hitler did not even inform the Japanese of his aggressive intentions. "We have only to kick in the door," Hitler boasted to one of his generals, "and the whole rotten structure will come crashing down!"

The Germans also chose to disregard the potential support of the millions of oppressed Soviet subjects who longed to throw off the communist yoke. The nineteenth-century German military authority, Carl von Clausewitz, had concluded after Napoléon's defeat that Russia could be conquered only from within. Indeed, it was internal divisiveness, culminating in the Bolshevik Revolution of 1917, as much as the kaiser's armies, that had doomed czarist Russia in World War I. Hitler's racism, however, precluded him from trying to reverse the revolution by winning over people open to the appeal of anticommunism and the promise of local independence.

Instead, Hitler intended to wage a ruthless campaign. He spoke of a "war of extermination." He proclaimed that German soldiers would not be bound by the rules of warfare of the Hague Convention or by the guidelines on the treatment of prisoners of the Geneva Convention, because the Soviet Union had not signed either agreement. "The war against Russia will be such that it cannot be fought in a gentlemanly fashion," he told a gathering of his senior commanders early in 1941. "This struggle is one of ideologies and racial differences and will have to be conducted with unprecedented, merciless, and unrelenting harshness."

Hitler issued a series of decrees for eradicating Russians. One fairly standard order empowered the army to summarily execute civilians who took up arms against the German invaders. Another, however, protected members of the Wehrmacht from the legal consequences of crimes against the Soviet population. And a so-called Commissar Decree required the liquidation of the Communist political commissars who shared control with military commanders in every unit of the Red Army.

The measures were to be carried out by the Wehrmacht as well as by the SS execution squads known as Einsatzgruppen, which would follow the conquering army to exterminate ideological and racial enemies. Many army officers were dismayed by the prospect of carrying out these gruesome orders, but their objections went no further than the army commander in chief, Brauchitsch, who saw no gain in provoking the Führer.

Through the late winter and into the spring of 1941, the Germans amassed their forces in East Prussia, Poland, and Rumania. Some 17,000 trains rolled

In the opening lines of the top-secret directive that launched Operation Barbarossa, Hitler boldly ordered his Wehrmacht to "crush Soviet Russia in a rapid campaign." The key to victory, he declared, would be a lightning advance to a line formed by the Dnieper and Dvina rivers (dotted red line) and the destruction of the bulk of the Red Army in western Russia through "daring operations led by deeply penetrating armored spearheads." Having smashed in the door, the invasion force would then direct its might toward Leningrad in the north and the Ukraine and the Donets Basin in the south. Moscow, the ultimate prize for the army's senior commanders, was to be taken only after the occupation of Leningrad and the conquest of the enemy's economic heartland. Then the triumphant Wehrmacht would pursue the remnants of the Soviet armed forces to the foothills of the Urals. The vaguely defined endpoint of the campaign would be the erection of a "barrier against Asiatic Russia" stretching from the mouth of the Volga River, at Astrakhan, north to Archangel, on the frigid White Sea (dashed red line).

An Ambitious Blueprint for Conquest

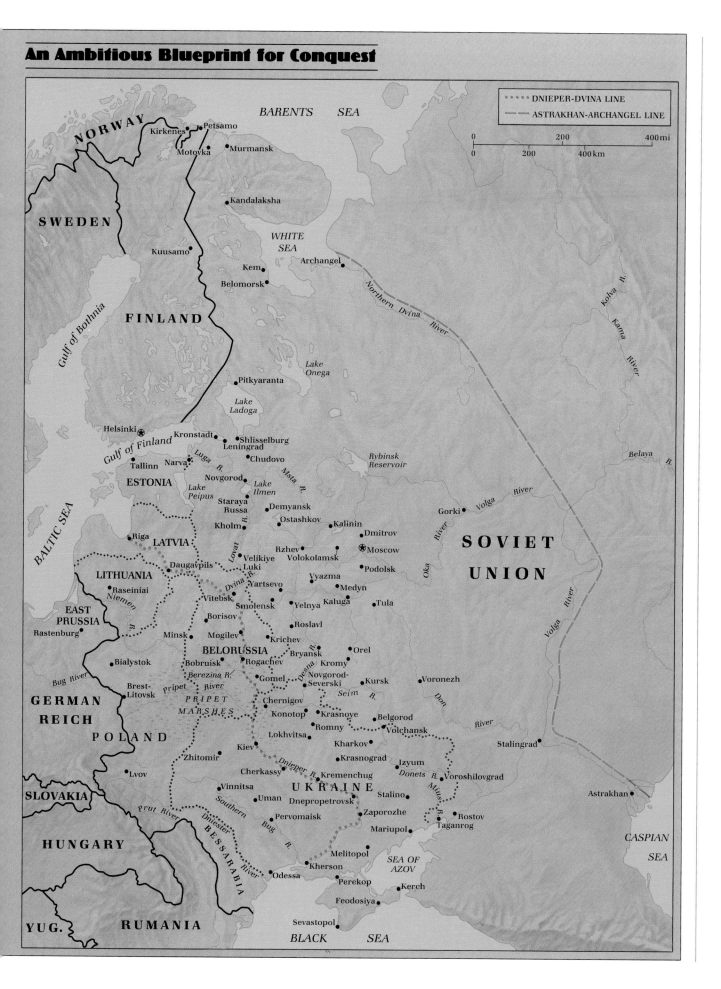

eastward bearing men and equipment. In April, part of the buildup was temporarily diverted southward for the brief campaign against Yugoslavia and Greece. This diversion did not seriously affect the launch of the Russian offensive, however. Originally targeted for the latter half of May, Barbarossa had to be postponed for about five weeks. The delay was attributable largely to shortages of vehicles in the newly formed panzer and motorized infantry divisions, and to heavy spring flooding in eastern Europe that rendered the border rivers impassable.

The movement eastward did not escape the attention of the Soviet dictator, Josef Stalin. Although the Germans staged a ruse by sending a score of second-line divisions westward to suggest preparations for an invasion of Britain, Stalin was not deceived. By late December 1940, the Russian military attaché in Berlin had received an anonymous letter containing the details of the Barbarossa directive issued one week earlier. Over the following months, dozens of warnings reached the Soviets. And throughout the spring, frequent border violations by German armed reconnaissance patrols and by specially equipped high-altitude spy planes kept the Russians on the alert.

Stalin appeared to ignore these indications of imminent invasion. He breathed not a word of public protest, forbade such discussions in the government-controlled press, and gave no evidence of mobilizing his armed forces. Well aware that mobilization by Czar Nicholas II had triggered the German declaration of war in 1914, Stalin was determined not to give Hitler a similar pretext. The Russian leader apparently believed that Hitler, unless he was provoked, would not attack without first issuing an ultimatum of some sort. In an attempt to appease the Führer, Stalin even continued shipments of grain and other commodities under a trade agreement with Germany. Meanwhile, he prudently negotiated a neutrality treaty with the Japanese.

Stalin was desperately trying to buy time for his armed forces. The Red Army was undergoing a modernization program to correct the deficiencies exposed during the Finnish war. At the same time, the recently appointed chief of the high command, General Georgy Zhukov, was rushing to implement his plan for an in-depth defense of the motherland. Zhukov's scheme was a variation on a Soviet offensive strategy developed during the 1930s. Rather than deploy the bulk of Soviet defenses near the border, it called for three successive lines of defense reaching more than 150 miles into the rear. Zhukov hoped that these zones of resistance would drain the energy of the German armored thrusts, enabling the last echelon, the strategic reserve, to mount a decisive counterattack.

The German invasion force that had taken up positions along the frontier by late spring outnumbered the estimated one million troops in the Soviet first line of defense by more than three to one. The German force consisted of 150 divisions: 19 of them were panzer divisions, and 14 were motorized infantry. The attackers' main objectives were to encircle the Red Army with deep armored thrusts and then to destroy it in the area lying between the frontier and a north-south line formed by the Dvina and Dnieper rivers, about 300 miles to the east.

As planned, the invaders were divided into three groups for the June invasion. Army Group North was the smallest force. Its thirty-one divisions were poised to move northeastward from East Prussia into Lithuania, clear the Baltic states, and capture Leningrad. Finland would provide support by attacking from the north with fourteen divisions two and a half weeks after the Germans moved. Army Group Center formed the largest force. Its fifty-seven divisions were to attack north of the Pripet Marshes, a vast swampland that stretched along the front for 150 miles. The group's two parallel columns would knife eastward into Belorussia, toward Smolensk and Moscow. Army Group South, comprising forty-eight divisions, was divided into two widely separated wings. The strong northern wing was to advance eastward along the southern edge of the Pripet Marshes into the Ukraine. Its targets were the Dnieper River and the city of Kiev. A smaller southern wing, made up of six German divisions and about 200,000 Rumanian troops, would cross the border from Rumania on July 1. Thus, all but fourteen divisions, held in OKH reserve, would be thrown into battle in the first fortnight.

Barbarossa began on schedule shortly after three in the morning on June 22. As darkness began to lift, thousands of German artillery pieces erupted in an awesome barrage. Hundreds of bombers streaked over the frontier to strike at Soviet airfields and troop concentrations situated as far as 200 miles east of the border. Then the panzers, their sides draped with sacks of rations and jerry cans of extra fuel, began to roll.

Curzio Malaparte, an Italian journalist accompanying Army Group South, described the scene in the early hours of the campaign: "The exhausts of the panzers belch out blue tongues of smoke. The air fills with a pungent bluish vapor that mingles with the damp green of the grass and with the golden reflection of the corn. Beneath the screaming arch of Stukas, the mobile columns of tanks resemble thin lines drawn with a pencil on the vast green slate of the Moldavian plain."

Many of the panzer spearheads and the infantry that followed had to cross formidable natural barriers. In the center, they faced the Bug River, which since 1939 had marked the frontier between German- and Soviet-

From an observation platform in a hardwood tree, German lookouts on the Soviet border search for signs of activity in June 1941, before the invasion. The Soviets stirred little, for Stalin feared that mobilization would provoke a German attack.

occupied Poland. Infantry in rubber boats braved Russian fire to clear the opposite bank and allow combat engineers to build pontoon bridges. Assault parties on foot and on motorcycles raced across existing bridges to surprise the defenders and disarm demolition charges before they could be ignited. The suddenness of the assaults stunned the Red Army outposts, and the Germans seized intact every essential bridge along the Bug.

North of the old frontier fortress at Brest-Litovsk, eighty tanks of the 18th Panzer Division crossed the Bug without benefit of a bridge. They simply rolled into the thirteen-foot-deep waters and crawled submerged across the bottom. These amphibious vehicles, originally intended for the invasion of Britain, were conventional Panzer IIIs and IVs specially outfitted for underwater use. A waterproof compound sealed all the exterior openings of the tank except the gap between hull and turret, which was enclosed by an inflatable rubber ring. Steel tubes, precursors of the snorkels later fitted to German U-boats, furnished fresh air and vented exhaust. The amphibious crossing received covering fire from fifty batteries of German artillery. "A magnificent spectacle," recalled the 18th Division commander, Major General Walther Nehring, "but rather pointless since the Russians had been clever enough to withdraw their troops from the border area."

As the panzers rammed through defenses from the Baltic Sea to the Carpathian Mountains, the Luftwaffe unleashed its aerial attacks. The priority targets were forward airfields that had been photographed by high-altitude reconnaissance planes. German pilots were pleased to discover that the scene at the airfields below bore a remarkable resemblance to the peacetime photographs they had studied. "We hardly believed our

German infantrymen paddle inflatable rafts across a river on the Russian border near a bridge being built to replace one destroyed by the Soviets. The demolition was an exception; striking suddenly, the Germans captured most bridges intact.

eyes," reported Captain Hans von Hahn, who flew an Me 109 fighter in the Lvov area. "Row after row of reconnaissance planes, bombers, and fighters stood lined up as if on parade."

German fragmentation bombs devastated the airfields. Chunks of steel from these little, four-pound missiles, which were known as "devil's eggs," ripped through the ranks of parked aircraft. At a base near Brest-Litovsk, the devil's eggs peppered a squadron of Soviet fighters trying in vain to get off the ground. Obsolete I-16 fighters with open cockpits struggled into the air only to be shot to pieces by the German Messerschmitts. Ponderous Soviet bombers took off unescorted in a brave effort to disrupt the invasion and were blown out of the sky by the dozens. Field Marshal Albert Kesselring of the Luftwaffe likened the work of picking them off to "infanticide."

By nightfall on invasion day, the Luftwaffe counted at least 1,800 Soviet aircraft destroyed, more than half of them on the ground. The panzer spearheads, supported by the Luftwaffe, had broken through on all fronts. Thousands of Russian soldiers had been taken prisoner; a dozen or more Soviet divisions had been shattered or swept aside. Only in the south did the Germans meet anything approaching organized resistance. Stalin had deployed the most troops there, mistakenly expecting the major drive to be mounted against agricultural and industrial objectives in the Ukraine.

The Luftwaffe had disrupted Red Army communications, which relied largely on telephone and telegraph lines, and had thereby contributed to the confusion and disorder that gripped the Soviet high command. General Zhukov had expected the first of his multiple lines of defense to give way gradually, buying time for successive lines to mount a counteroffensive. He had not foreseen blows as swift and as punishing as those the Germans delivered. Stalin himself was so shocked by the devastating breakthrough that he failed to issue orders to counterattack until four hours after the German attack had begun.

From Berlin, Hitler followed the first day's spectacular results with mounting excitement. On the eve of the invasion, he had written to his Italian partner, Benito Mussolini, to inform him for the first time of the impending attack and to express his delight at feeling "spiritually free"—of being "delivered from this torment" of Germany's twenty-two-month alliance with the Soviet Union. On June 24, two days after the invasion, Hitler arrived by train at his new headquarters, which he called Wolfsschanze, or Wolf's Lair, near Rastenburg in East Prussia. Here, in a compound of wooden huts and concrete blockhouses hidden in a thick forest, Hitler joked that the mosquitoes were so big he would have to call in the Luftwaffe.

East of Hitler's headquarters, Army Group North, under Field Marshal

German bicycle troops enter a burning Russian village during the first week of the invasion. The Soviet terrain proved too difficult for bicycles; the soldiers soon abandoned them and continued the advance on foot.

Wilhelm Ritter von Leeb, was bound for Leningrad. Its Panzer Group 4, flanked by two armies of infantry, crossed the Memel River. On the left, the Eighteenth Army skirted the Baltic coast, heading for the old Latvian capital and seaport of Riga; on the right, the Sixteenth Army provided flank protection by maintaining contact with Army Group Center. In the middle, the LVI Panzer Corps had sped fifty miles on invasion day to seize the gateway to the Baltic hinterland—the road and rail viaduct over the giant Dubysa Gorge near the Lithuanian village of Airogala.

While this armored column faced only scattered resistance, the other corps in Panzer Group 4 found a surprise in its path. On the evening of June 23, near the village of Raseiniai, the XLI Panzer Corps encountered more than 300 enemy tanks. Many of them were heavy tanks whose capabilities

The Wehrmacht's Armored Workhorses

A world stunned by the brutal swiftness of blitzkrieg could scarcely imagine flaws in the Wehrmacht's legendary armored legions. Yet by the end of the French campaign, the panzers had all too often found themselves outgunned and under-armored. Victory resulted more from superior tactics and organization than from the machines.

Blinded by the succession of triumphs and hobbled by sluggish production, Germany's warlords were slow to upgrade their tanks in the months before Barbarossa. Although Panzer I and II models were phased out at an accelerated pace, little was done to improve the armor and killing power of the heavier, but still relatively thin-skinned,

Panzer III and IV. The Panzer III's original 37-mm gun—reviled as an impotent "door knocker"—was replaced with a 50-mm cannon *(above)*, but on the battlefields of the Soviet Union even that would prove hardly more than a stopgap.

Despite these lapses, the Germans were quick to capitalize on a powerful addition to their armored arsenal—the *Sturmgeschütz*, or assault gun *(right)*. Consisting of a 75-mm howitzer mounted on a Panzer III chassis, the hybrid weapon had proved its worth both as mobile artillery and as a tank killer during the 1940 campaigns. Its numbers were expanded tenfold for the storming of Russia, where every piece of armor would be sorely needed.

Panzer IIIG

The sturdy, reliable Panzer III, backbone of German armored regiments in 1941, was well liked by its crew of five. This one belonged to the 3d Panzer Division, part of General Heinz Guderian's Panzer Group 2. Its high-velocity 50-mm gun had greater penetrating power than the 75-mm on the Panzer IV but still came up short in head-to-head duels with Russian T-34s.

Sturmgeschütz IIID

Organized into independent detachments, assault guns such as the one below usually accompanied infantry units to provide close-in fire support. Their four-man crews included a commander, gunner, driver, and loader-radio operator. A low, hard-to-target profile and thick frontal armor offset the disadvantage of the limited-traverse gun mounted in the hull.

were largely unknown to the Germans. Called Kliment Voroshilovs, or KVs, after a hero of the Revolution, these monsters were superior in many ways to the Wehrmacht's best. Weighing more than forty tons, the KV-1 was twice as heavy as the Panzer III and Panzer IV and had armor plate two to three times as thick, but its top speed was only a few miles per hour slower. Moreover, the KV-1 and the even-heavier KV-2 rode on wide treads that gave firmer traction in the sand and mud of the northern front. "Our companies opened fire at about 800 yards, but it was ineffective," wrote the chronicler of the 1st Panzer Division. "We moved closer and closer to the enemy, who for his part continued to approach us unconcerned. Very soon we were facing each other at 50 to 100 yards. A fantastic exchange of fire took place without any visible German success. The Russian tanks continued to advance, and our armor-piercing shells simply bounced off them."

Field Marshal Wilhelm Ritter von Leeb *(left foreground)*, accompanied by officers of his Army Group North, was an exacting commander with a reputation as a skilled strategist. A devout Catholic, Leeb rejected nazism but served Hitler with the loyalty of an old-school officer.

For more than two days, the clash of armor resounded. The Soviet tanks withstood shells from antitank guns as well as from the panzers' 50-mm and 75-mm cannon; one KV-2 took more than seventy hits, and not one shot pierced its thick armor. The panzers immobilized some of the Russian tanks by first firing at the vulnerable treads, then bringing up artillery to pound the stalled giants at close range. Combat engineers attacked others on foot with satchels of explosives. Finally, on the morning of June 26, the corps commander, Lieut. General Georg-Hans Reinhardt, a veteran of the blitzkrieg in France, taught the Red Army tankers a lesson in tactics. While one division held the front, another counterattacked from the flank, driving the enemy tanks into a swamp. The Soviets, who had shown their inexperience by mounting uncoordinated frontal assaults, lost nearly 200 tanks.

During the same morning, the LVI Panzer Corps raced ahead toward a vital objective farther to the northeast. The corps was commanded by Lieut. General Erich von Manstein, a brilliant strategist who had helped devise the plan for the invasion of France in 1940 and who was now proving himself equally capable in the field. Shouting from his command tank "Keep going! Keep going!" any time his subordinates faltered, he had driven his panzers 200 miles in four days and destroyed seventy enemy tanks. The goal of this thrust was the Dvina River and the crossings at the Latvian city of Daugavpils, a key rail center between the border and Leningrad. By seizing the 250-yard-long road and rail bridges there, Manstein would keep the route to Leningrad open and cut off Soviet forces south of the Dvina.

Manstein halted his column about four miles from the bridges. Subterfuge would now substitute for speed. To avoid alarming the Soviets and to keep them from blowing up the bridges, he dispatched about two dozen men of the Brandenburg Regiment, a commando unit specially trained for such missions. Disguised as wounded Red Army soldiers, the Brandenburgers rode forward in four captured trucks driven by Russian-speaking Germans also wearing Soviet uniforms. The convoy blended in with Red

Curious German soldiers swarm over a huge Soviet KV-2 tank captured near the city of Dubno on June 29. Writing on the turret indicates that gunners of the General Göring Regiment had knocked out the behemoth.

Army traffic so smoothly that Russian soldiers at the roadside waved to them and exchanged greetings.

Near the river, the convoy split up. One truck headed for the railroad bridge. The occupants had to fight across after Soviet sentries saw through the ruse and opened fire. The Brandenburgers cut the wires to the demolition charges on the bridge, although one charge went off accidentally, causing minor damage. Their colleagues in the three other trucks attacked the road bridge. They ran over a sentry who challenged the first truck, raced across to dismantle the explosives attached to the far side of the span, and shot the remaining sentries.

These Brandenburgers paid for their audacity moments later, when Russian soldiers rushed the bridge from either side. Six of the Germans, including the leader, First Lieutenant Wolfram Knaak, were killed, and many of the rest were wounded. German reinforcements arrived in time to rescue the survivors and seize both bridges intact. Soon, Manstein's panzers were clattering to the far bank and routing the Russians from the streets of Daugavpils. The Brandenburgers' coup at the Dvina crossings, 300 miles short of Leningrad, was a fitting climax to the drive by Manstein's panzers. "The impetuous dash" to the Dvina, he wrote later, was "the fulfillment of a tank-force commander's dreams."

Manstein's dreams soon dissolved in frustration and hard slogging. His corps was ordered to wait at the Dvina bridgehead for six days, until the rest of the panzer group and the infantry caught up. Then, as the German spearhead continued northeastward, the panzers encountered tougher Russian resistance and marshy terrain less and less suitable for armor. Despite Army Group North's impressive progress during the first week, it had failed in its mission of trapping large numbers of enemy troops south of the Dvina: Only 6,000 had been taken prisoner as the Red Army withdrew from the Baltic states to the familiar ground of old Russia.

Disagreements over tactics in the German high command produced further problems and delays. Was it too risky for the panzer spearheads to outdistance the infantry and advance with flanks exposed? Should the Baltic seaports be secured before the panzers drove on to Leningrad? Such questions generated confusion and bitterness at every level of command. Hitler, too, began meddling in tactical decisions from his headquarters at Rastenburg. All the same, Army Group North forged ahead. During the second week in July, the panzer spearheads pierced the fortifications of the Stalin Line, which marked the pre-1940 Soviet frontier. And on July 14, Reinhardt's XLI Panzer Corps crossed the Luga River and established a bridgehead less than eighty miles from Leningrad (map, page 51).

On the other flank of the German offensive, Army Group South was

An SS unit, its equipment and supplies drawn by horses, crosses the Western Dvina River over a makeshift bridge on the way to Leningrad. Despite its reputation as a mechanized force, the German army used nearly 625,000 draft horses in the invasion of the Soviet Union.

making progress, though less rapidly than the forces to the north. The Soviet units in the western Ukraine were the largest, best led, and best equipped in the Red Army—a "most determined adversary," conceded Field Marshal Gerd von Rundstedt, the veteran German commander on the southern front. The two wings of Army Group South were to converge eventually at the great bend in the Dnieper River south of Kiev, the old capital of the Ukraine and the Soviet Union's third largest city. On the right, poised in Rumania, the German Eleventh Army, reinforced by Rumanian troops, did little more than establish bridgeheads across the Prut River through the end of June. It was positioned to stop a possible counterthrust by the Red Army to seize the Rumanian oil fields at Ploesti. Meanwhile, the wing on the left—Panzer Group 1, flanked by two armies of infantry, the Sixth and the Seventeenth—attacked from southern Poland and ran into the fiercest resistance offered by the Soviets during the first week of fighting.

The panzers slowly fought forward in a series of engagements against stubborn enemy armor. On June 23, having penetrated fifty miles into the Ukraine, the five panzer divisions under General Ewald von Kleist encountered the heavy KV tanks that menaced their colleagues in the Baltic region. They also came up against a new medium-weight model, the T-34.

The appearance of the T-34, which was both heavier and faster than the Panzer III and IV, momentarily stunned the Germans. In their first meeting with the T-34, antitank-gun crews from the 16th Panzer Division could count their 37-mm shells ricocheting off the sloping armor plate of the enemy machine at a range of less than 100 yards. Again, however, the poor training of the Soviet tank crews tipped the scales in favor of the panzers. Their commanders squandered armor in uncoordinated attacks, violating General Heinz Guderian's maxim of concentration—"Not driblets, but mass." Moreover, the gunner in the T-34 also served as commander of the four-man crew, a dual function that interfered with efficient and rapid fire. For their part, the Germans quickly learned to isolate the new tanks by first knocking out the older ones. They then pounced on the KVs and T-34s with combination attacks by planes, panzers, and artillery—including 88-mm flak guns fired horizontally.

Kleist's panzers broke through after a week of running battle, but they failed to encircle their enemy as intended. The Russian armor and infantry retreated more or less intact and regrouped 150 miles to the east, behind the fortifications of the Stalin Line. Even there, 100 miles west and southwest of Kiev, the Germans breached the defenses on July 7, but they had to keep hammering away with panzers and air attacks for several more days before forcing another Russian withdrawal to the Dnieper.

As they rumbled forward, the panzers and the supporting infantry deployed on their flanks faced problems other than the enemy immediately in front. Pockets of Red Army soldiers remained in action up to 100 miles behind the German spearheads, and their attacks from the rear were a constant and lethal irritant. Entire Russian divisions hid in the wooded swampland of the Pripet Marshes, on the north side of Kleist's advance, and repeatedly attacked the German flank. Once, they temporarily severed the main supply route of Panzer Group 1. In a clash that lasted two days, a German infantry battalion lost 170 men dead and wounded—nearly one-fourth of its effective strength.

German planners had neither foreseen such problems nor anticipated the difficulties of terrain and climate in the Ukraine. The roads designated by the Wehrmacht as *Rollbahnen*, or highways, were distressingly scarce, and the available maps of Russia were grossly inaccurate. "The roads that were marked nice and red and thick on a map turned out to be tracks," Rundstedt later recalled. Sudden thunderstorms turned the tracks into quagmires knee-deep in black, sticky clay that the troops nicknamed Buna, after the synthetic rubber on which much of the Wehrmacht rode. When the fabled black earth of the Ukraine dried, it rose in clouds of fine dust that clogged lungs and engines and challenged the soldiers' sanity by creating apparitions. On one occasion, an entire company of German motorcyclists dived for roadside ditches and then climbed out sheepishly when the enemy tank looming out of the dust resolved itself into a peasant's wagon piled high with manure.

The assaults of mud, dust, and enemy resilience also slowed Rundstedt's southern wing as it advanced from Rumania, but its main problems were a lack of tanks and air support. The German and Rumanian troops crossed the Prut River in strength on July 1 and moved northeastward through Bessarabia, the former Rumanian province that the Soviets had absorbed

Ukrainian villagers offer a plate of bread and salt, the traditional gift of welcome, to Germans advancing into southern Russia. Like other ethnic groups hostile to Stalin's rule, Ukrainians initially viewed the Germans more as liberators than as conquerors.

Tanks and other armored vehicles of General Ewald von Kleist's Panzer Group 1 await the signal to attack across a vast plain in

the Ukraine. In the distance, plumes of smoke billow from a bombarded Russian town.

the previous year. The soldiers were supposed to aid in the encirclement of the Soviet troops southeast of Kiev, but their snail-like progress—an average of eight miles a day—put them hopelessly behind schedule.

Meanwhile, the northern wing ranged far ahead. A column of Kleist's panzers had punched through the Stalin Line and raced eastward. By July 10, the tanks had moved to within a dozen miles of Kiev—but no closer. Hitler had intervened. He forbade the German armor to enter the city and ordered Kleist to turn south to cut off the retreating Soviets.

It was in the center of the long Russian front that the German invaders achieved their most dramatic victories. Army Group Center, the most powerful of the three German spearheads, consisted of Panzer Group 2 and Panzer Group 3, and two infantry armies, the Fourth and the Ninth, all under the command of Field Marshal Fedor von Bock. The panzer wedges attacked separately out of Poland, roughly 125 miles apart, and drove into Belorussia, intending to converge later in a giant pincer movement.

In less than a week, the panzer columns—Panzer Group 2, commanded by General Heinz Guderian, and Panzer Group 3, commanded by General Hermann Hoth—penetrated nearly 250 miles beyond the border. On June 27, their jaws snapped shut from north and south at the city of Minsk, enclosing nearly half a million Soviet troops in the first of the so-called battles of encirclement. A day later, the two German infantry armies closed a smaller ring east of Bialystok, about 100 miles inside Soviet territory.

Many of the trapped Red Army units fought with fanatical zeal to break out. The men of Guderian's 29th Motorized Infantry Division watched in astonishment as the Russians repeatedly mounted suicidal human-wave attacks. Linking arms and holding long, fixed bayonets rigidly in front of them like lances, they charged, roaring defiance, into the certain death of German machine-gun fire.

In addition to killing thousands of the enemy, the Germans captured 300,000 prisoners and destroyed or seized 2,500 tanks in the two pockets. The Soviet high command had been willing to countenance losses initially, but this was too much. The Red Army commander on this front, General Dimitri Pavlov, was summoned to Moscow on June 30, along with his principal staff officers. They were executed.

From the Minsk encirclement, the panzer spearheads rolled eastward under a canopy of Luftwaffe fighters. On June 30, near Bobruisk, waves of Soviet bombers attempted to break through the German air cover in a desperate attempt to disrupt Guderian's Panzer Group 2. Again, the bombers were without benefit of fighter escort, and they ran into the Me 109s of Jagdgeschwader 51. The Germans shot down 114 planes that day, be-

Defiance in an Eighteenth-Century Citadel

A gateway to the Citadel at Brest-Litovsk shows the effects of German bombardment during the battle for the fortress.

In their rush to slice deeply into the Soviet Union during the early hours of Operation Barbarossa, German panzers bypassed the old fortress city of Brest-Litovsk, which was situated at the center of Russia's border defenses. The job of capturing the isolated stronghold was assigned to the 45th Infantry Division of Field Marshal Günther Hans von Kluge's potent Fourth Army.

The Wehrmacht's assault surprised the outnumbered Soviet garrison, and by the second day of the campaign, virtually all of Brest-Litovsk was in German hands. Some 3,000 Red Army survivors, however, holed up inside the Citadel—a military compound that occupied four islands at the confluence of the Bug and Mukhavets rivers. Protected by turreted ramparts and water-filled moats, the eighteenth-century complex appeared woefully outmoded, but the walls proved to be remarkably resistant to artillery fire, and even repeated strikes by Luftwaffe dive bombers failed to subdue the defiant holdouts.

Once German infantry units had breached the Citadel's walls, they had to advance up hazardous, narrow streets that were enfiladed by camouflaged Russian machine guns and artillery. Every barracks room and cellar had to be painstakingly searched for defenders, many of whom were determined to fight to the death (*following pages*).

German infantry moves warily along a street inside the Citadel. Russian snipers exacted a heavy toll: On the first day of the assault on the complex, the Wehrmacht lost 21 officers and 290 enlisted men killed.

Above, soldiers of the 45th Infantry Division pick their way along one of the Citadel's battlements. The two-mile-square fortress confronted the Germans with a labyrinth of defenses that made a coordinated assault impossible.

At left, Soviet defenders, hands raised in surrender, are rousted from a dugout in the Citadel. The battle for Brest-Litovsk dragged on for a week, then pockets of Russians holed up in the fortress. It took the Germans a month to clear the last of them.

On July 20, 1941, a lone resister carved a defiant epitaph on a barracks basement wall: "I am dying, but I won't surrender! Farewell, Motherland!"

coming the first fighter group in the Luftwaffe to destroy 1,000 enemy aircraft. The group commander, Colonel Werner Mölders, scored five kills, bringing his own total to eighty-two, the highest in the Luftwaffe.

Back in East Prussia, Halder, chief of the army high command and principal advocate of the drive on Moscow, savored the dazzling successes of the center. On June 30, Halder's fifty-seventh birthday, Hitler himself came to tea, a gesture of approbation all the more significant in light of their previous differences over strategy. Three days later, as Guderian's lead panzers approached Rogachev, on the Dnieper, 115 miles southeast of Minsk, the usually cautious Halder arrived at a premature conclusion. He asserted in his diary on July 3 that the objective of destroying the bulk of the Red Army west of the Dvina and Dnieper rivers had already been achieved. Although hard fighting lay ahead, he wrote, "It is probably no overstatement to say the Russian campaign has been won in the space of two weeks." The next day, Hitler echoed Halder's words over lunch with his foreign minister, Joachim von Ribbentrop, and enlarged on his plans for colonizing a conquered Russia.

In their euphoria, the leaders of the Reich once again underestimated the strength and tenacity of the Red Army. All along the line, Soviet units cut off by the rapid advance of the panzers continued to strike fiercely against the German infantry that lagged behind the armor. The Russian soldiers were motivated in more ways than one: by loyalty to the motherland, by fear of imprisonment by the Germans, and by the threats of their own political commissars, who shot laggards and deserters.

A statue of Vladimir Ilich Lenin, father of the Russian Revolution, lies broken in the main square of Minsk after the Germans captured the city on June 26.

Soviet prisoners await escort to the rear from a collection point near Minsk. The German encirclement of the Bialystok and Minsk pockets ensnared 300,000 Russian captives, most of whom would die of disease or starve while in German custody.

At the tips of the panzer spearheads, as well as in the rear, were warning signs that the Soviets were far from beaten. The powerful new Russian tanks were now appearing on the central front. On July 3, the day Halder waxed so optimistically in his diary, one of Guderian's divisions, the 18th Panzer, came under attack from medium T-34s and heavy KV-2s on the main highway from Minsk to Moscow near the Berezina River. Afterward, General Walther Nehring, the division commander, counted eleven hits in the plating of a KV, none of which had penetrated.

During the following few days, German tankers prevailed over the superior Soviet machines in a series of engagements—but only because of German tactical experience and the improvisational skills of the supporting infantry. Soldiers of the German 101st Rifle Regiment demonstrated their ability to cope with the KVs in a clash with one of the giants on July 7. They lashed together hand grenades and lobbed them at the tank's gun turret. After the turret was disabled, a lieutenant jumped aboard the tank and another soldier tossed him a stick grenade. He caught it, pulled the pin, shoved it in the thick barrel of the vehicle's 152-mm gun, and jumped clear. The grenade set off the shell in the breech of the gun, and the explosion blew open the hatch. Another German finished off the tank by hurling an explosive charge through the open hatch from twenty-five feet away.

Perhaps the most dangerous threat to the German offensive was neither the Red Army's fanatical tenacity nor its formidable new tanks. It was instead the indecision and dissension that continued to afflict the German leadership. The commanders, from Hitler on down, could not agree on strategic objectives or tactical means.

At the center of the storm rode the commander of Panzer Group 2, Heinz Guderian. One of the authors of blitzkrieg theory, he had helped prove the strategy as a panzer commander in Poland and France. Now he was adding to his reputation for flamboyance and daring: He ordered all his vehicles painted with a large white letter *G*, and he led his panzers from the head of the column, rather than from a headquarters in the rear. In one instance, Guderian himself gallantly operated the machine gun of his armored command vehicle to break through an enemy roadblock. The general cut such an exalted figure that his Luftwaffe liaison officer likened him to the "war god himself." He also had a reputation for arrogance that had earned him the nickname *Brausewetter*, or Hothead.

The early days of July found Guderian and Hoth, the commander of Panzer Group 3, determined to increase their remarkable advances by forging even deeper into Soviet territory. They were in a hurry to reach the Dnieper River and the city of Smolensk, the first major objective of Army

After smashing through the Soviet border defenses, three German army groups thrust eastward into the enemy's heartland. Four panzer groups (*dark red*) spearheaded the attack, and eight armies of infantry (*light red*) followed in their wake and along their flanks. In the north, Leeb's army group swiftly overran Lithuania and Latvia, and by mid-July his panzers were poised along the Luga River for a climactic drive on Leningrad. Meanwhile, the two panzer groups in Bock's Army Group Center teamed up to encircle the Soviet forces in Belorussia. Leaving the infantry to finish off the trapped Russian armies, Bock's armored vanguard pressed across the Dnieper-Dvina line, capturing Smolensk, two-thirds of the way to Moscow, on July 16. On the southern flank, Rundstedt's group ran into fierce resistance, first near the frontier and later along the Stalin Line. Finally, during the second week of July, the Russian line broke, and the Germans raced across the Ukraine toward Kiev.

Thrusts into the Heartland

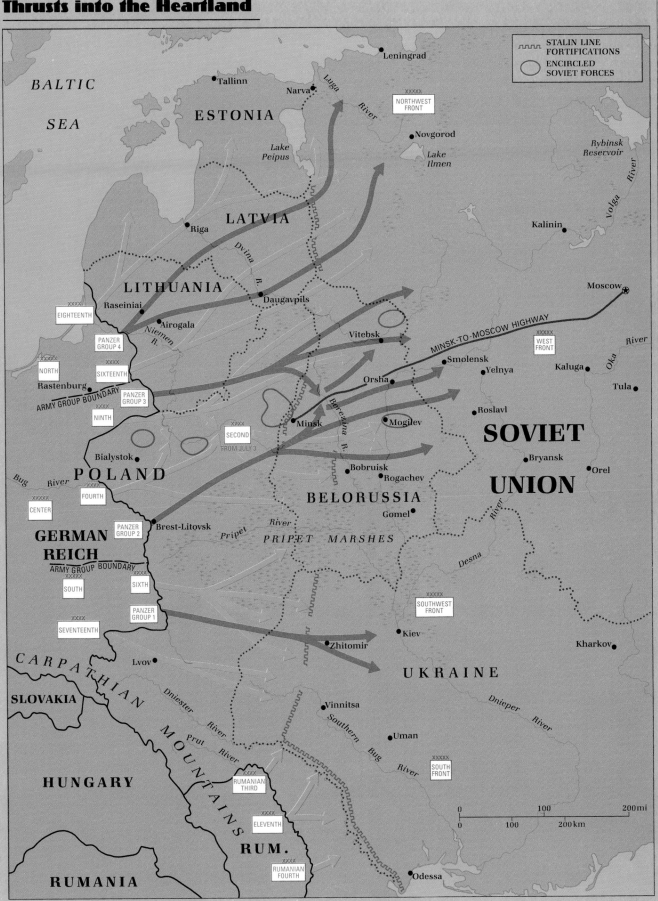

STALIN LINE
FORTIFICATIONS
ENCIRCLED
SOVIET FORCES

BALTIC
SEA

Leningrad

Tallinn
Narva

ESTONIA

Luga
River

NORTHWEST
FRONT

Novgorod

Lake
Peipus

Lake
Ilmen

Rybinsk
Reservoir

Volga River

LATVIA

Riga

Dvina R.

Kalinin

LITHUANIA

Daugavpils

Moscow

EIGHTEENTH

Raseiniai

Airogala

Niemen R.

Vitebsk

MINSK-TO-MOSCOW HIGHWAY

WEST
FRONT

Oka River

PANZER
GROUP 4

NORTH

SIXTEENTH

Smolensk

Yelnya

Kaluga

Tula

Rastenburg

Orsha

ARMY GROUP BOUNDARY

PANZER
GROUP 3

Berezina R.

Roslavl

SOVIET

NINTH

Minsk

Mogilev

Bialystok

SECOND
FROM JULY 3

Bryansk

UNION

Orel

Bug River

POLAND

Bobruisk

Rogachev

BELORUSSIA

CENTER

FOURTH

Gomel

Pripet River

PRIPET MARSHES

Desna River

GERMAN
REICH

PANZER
GROUP 2

Brest-Litovsk

ARMY GROUP BOUNDARY

SOUTH

SIXTH

SOUTHWEST
FRONT

SEVENTEENTH

PANZER
GROUP 1

Kiev

Kharkov

Lvov

Zhitomir

UKRAINE

CARPATHIAN

Dniester River

Vinnitsa

Dnieper River

SLOVAKIA

Prut River

Southern Bug River

Uman

MOUNTAINS

SOUTH
FRONT

HUNGARY

RUMANIAN
THIRD

ELEVENTH

0   100   200mi

RUM.

0   100   200km

RUMANIA

RUMANIAN
FOURTH

Odessa

Group Center. Hitler and others were more concerned with the reduction of the pockets at Bialystok and Minsk. They favored holding back the panzer groups to help the infantry.

Privately, the army high command hoped that the panzer chiefs would race impetuously ahead. To mollify Hitler, however, Halder and Brauchitsch pretended to rein in Guderian and Hoth by subordinating them to a conservative commander. On July 3, Field Marshal Günther Hans von Kluge took the two panzer groups into his newly created Fourth Panzer Army. Kluge's infantry units were transferred to the control of the Second Army headquarters staff, under General Maximilian Freiherr von Weichs.

Kluge was an old-line artillery officer, an energetic fifty-eight-year-old Prussian whose play-on-words nickname, *Kluger Hans*, or Clever Hans, recognized his political acumen. Guderian had served under Kluge in France and disliked him personally and professionally. He referred to Kluge in a letter from Russia as a "brake on progress." Almost immediately, Kluge clashed with his new subordinates. Guderian and Hoth disobeyed

Above, General Heinz Guderian's staff car, emblazoned with his personal *G*, attempts to cross a makeshift causeway at the head of his panzer column during the advance toward Moscow.

General Guderian *(right)* confers with his superior, Field Marshal Kluge *(seated)*, at a command post on the central front. The two officers clashed over Guderian's aggressive tactics.

his orders by refusing to hold back divisions to prevent breakouts from the pocket around Minsk. When both generals rationalized their moves as mistakes in the transmission of orders, Kluge accused them of fomenting a "generals' conspiracy" and threatened them with courts-martial.

Undeterred, Guderian decided on his own to break out across the Dnieper and drive the final 100 miles to Smolensk. On July 9, the day before the planned operation, Kluge appeared at Guderian's headquarters and angrily confronted his rebellious subordinate. He ordered that the crossing by the panzers be delayed until the infantry arrived. Guderian argued

heatedly that the enemy was reinforcing its defenses across the Dnieper. It would take nearly a fortnight for the German infantry to reach the river, he contended, and by that time the Soviet line would be too strong to break.

Guderian wrote later that he told Kluge, as a last resort, that "preparations had already gone too far to be canceled." He argued that panzers from two of his corps were "massed on their jumping-off positions" and could only be kept there "for a limited length of time before the Russian air force must find them and attack them." Guderian went on to voice his confidence that the attack would succeed and to predict that "this operation would decide the Russian campaign in this very year."

Kluge retorted: "Your operations always hang by a thread!" But beaten down by Guderian's arguments and aware that the panzer chief had the secret backing of the army high command, Kluge reluctantly gave in. The panzers resumed their advance on Smolensk on July 10. Guderian's armored force took the southern route, bridging the Dnieper at three points;

While Vitebsk burns around them, men of the 20th Panzer Division take a break to eat and drink. As part of the Soviets' scorched-earth policy, Russian soldiers had set fire to the buildings before they withdrew.

German soldiers break down a door during mopping-up operations in Smolensk. The city fell to Army Group Center on July 16, but in the industrial suburbs, police and workers' militia units continued to wage a desperate, house-by-house resistance.

Hoth's panzers attacked on the north via Vitebsk, on the Dvina River. Against increasing resistance, the columns averaged less than fifteen miles a day. Nonetheless, on July 16, after bitter house-to-house fighting, Guderian's 29th Motorized Infantry Division seized Smolensk. At the same time, Hoth's panzer spearhead bypassed Smolensk and converged on the city from thirty miles to the north, virtually completing the double envelopment of two Soviet armies.

The German goals now seemed within reach. In the north and in the south, the army groups were in striking distance of their objectives, Leningrad and Kiev. And on the central front, the panzers had gone even farther, advancing 450 miles in the twenty-five days since Barbarossa had begun. The Russian capital now lay only about 225 miles away, and Guderian's tankers posted hand-painted signs along the concrete highway east of Smolensk. The markers pointed the way "to Moscow." ✚

Victories and Vacillation

During the night of July 22, 1941, less than a week after the capture of Smolensk, the Germans attacked Moscow—not from the ground, but from the air. Responding to Hitler's exhortation to level the Soviet capital, the Luftwaffe launched 127 twin-engine bombers carrying 104 tons of high-explosive bombs and 46,000 incendiaries. About twenty miles west of their target, the bombers encountered the blue-white flash of searchlights. Then came the crump-crump of antiaircraft guns. The bursts of flak and the blinding glare of the searchlights disrupted the German formations. Bombs fell scattershot across the city. Incendiaries hit the Kremlin roof, but layers of sturdy tiles dating from the seventeenth century kept the small bombs from penetrating and doing much damage.

The July raid, and others that followed through the rest of the year, failed to make a significant impact on the campaign. The Germans had neither enough bombers nor enough bombs to do more than briefly terrorize Moscow's civilian population. On the ground, however, German panzers had rolled to within 200 miles of the capital, and the citizens expected them to arrive at any moment. Yet as the summer wore on, no tanks appeared. Germany's military leaders were locked in a struggle over strategic objectives, and their drive on the Soviet capital stalled while they squabbled over the priorities of Barbarossa.

The debate over objectives had intensified as the panzers of Army Group Center raced beyond Smolensk. Hitler was delighted that the armored spearheads had penetrated nearly 500 miles, but the farther they reached, the more he fretted. He worried about the security of their flanks and feared that the wide gaps opening between tanks and infantry—more than 100 miles in parts of General Heinz Guderian's sector, for example—would defeat the concept of encirclement, which had been designed to surround and destroy entire Russian armies.

Hitler expressed his concerns in Directive 33, issued on July 19, and a supplemental Directive 33a, passed down four days later. In them, he called for the bombing of Moscow and ordered a virtual halt to the overland drive

Beneath the onion-shaped domes of a Russian Orthodox church, flames consume a village in the Ukraine. As Soviet forces fell back, they carried out Stalin's order to burn everything that the advancing Germans might use.

toward the capital. He decreed that the two panzer groups of Army Group Center were to be diverted to the flanks. General Hermann Hoth's Panzer Group 3 was to head north to join the assault on Leningrad; Guderian's Panzer Group 2 was to turn south to help conquer the Ukraine.

Hitler's orders should not have surprised his subordinates. The original plan for Barbarossa called for a pause in the march to Moscow and a diversion of armor north and south. But all along, the chief of the army high command, Franz Halder, and other advocates of an all-out push against Moscow had blithely assumed that they could talk the Führer out of this notion when the time came.

Now the time had come, and the familiar debate over Barbarossa's objectives—Moscow or the flank targets of Leningrad and the Ukraine?—simmered toward a boil. Hitler and Halder were the chief protagonists. Halder formally protested Hitler's directives while privately pouring vitriol into his diary and personal letters. "The Führer's constant interference is becoming a regular nuisance," he wrote. "He's playing warlord again and bothering us with absurd ideas."

Streaking tracer bullets and parachute flares illuminate the Moscow night as the Russians fight back against a German air raid. *Life* magazine photographer Margaret Bourke-White took the picture above on July 26, 1941, from the roof of the National Hotel. At right, Muscovite women and children bed down in the Mayakovskaya subway station, which has been converted into an air-raid shelter.

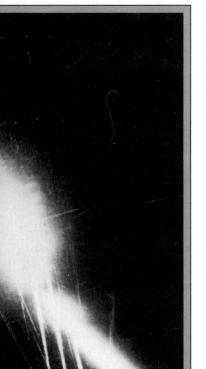

Halder did agree in part with Hitler's position. He recognized the need to protect the flanks of Army Group Center and recommended to Hitler that the tank columns pause until the infantry caught up. Nevertheless, he considered Hitler's plan to shift the focus of the offensive from Moscow to Leningrad and the Ukraine a disaster. His protests persuaded Hitler on July 28 to postpone the diversion of the panzer groups to the flanks, but the Führer kept the brakes on the thrust toward Moscow.

The argument, however, was far from over. For weeks, tremors from the angry clash at the top would reverberate down the chain of command to the very tips of the panzer spearheads. There, the diehard advocates of blitzkrieg, such as Heinz Guderian, would connive to get their way.

While senior officers vacillated, the troops of Army Group Center bumped into the fiercest opposition of the month-old campaign. In mid-July, after one of Guderian's divisions had captured Smolensk, the lead tanks of Hoth's Panzer Group 3 bypassed the city to the north. Then they hooked to the right, intending to link up with Guderian's tanks and seal off the strong Soviet forces east of Smolensk. A German staff officer, however, recalled that it was appallingly difficult country for tank movement. "Great virgin forests, widespread swamps, terrible roads and bridges, neither strong enough to bear the weight of tanks," he wrote. "The resistance also stiffened, and the Russians began to cover their front with minefields. It was easy for them to block the way because there were so few roads."

The Red Army also unleashed against Hoth's armor one of its secret weapons—the Katyusha, or Little Kate. Named for the heroine of a popular love song, it consisted of rockets that were fired from truck-mounted rails and had a range of up to four miles. The first rocket salvos were hurled against the 5th Infantry Division at Rudnia, northeast of Smolensk. Whining eerily as they streaked through the air and showering shrapnel upon impact, the rockets terrified not only the Germans, but also front-line Russians, who for security reasons had not been told of the weapon's existence. Because of the sound and the pipelike rails, the Germans dubbed the new weapon the "Stalin organ."

While Hoth tried to envelop Smolensk from the north, part of Guderian's panzer group swept past the city in the south. Instead of turning north to meet Hoth immediately, however, Guderian sent his 10th Panzer Division farther east, to Yelnya, a rail junction on a commanding ridge about forty-five miles southeast of Smolensk. Guderian had Moscow, not encirclement, on his mind, and he saw the high ground at Yelnya as the springboard for an attack on the capital. His panzers took Yelnya late on July 19 after a daylong battle. The effort to seize and hold the city prevented Guderian from moving north in force to link up with Hoth and close the circle.

Determined to smash the developing ring around Smolensk, the Russians mounted a fierce counterattack on July 23. A score of fresh divisions from the reserve joined the battle, pushing from the east and southeast. At the same time, tens of thousands of troops from two trapped Soviet armies fought desperately to break out of the unfinished circle. That night, at least five divisions slipped through the gap between Hoth and Guderian in the east. The Luftwaffe estimated that more than 100,000 Russians escaped from the Smolensk pocket.

Hitler kept informed on the leakage, which loomed large in his decision to slow the advance against Moscow. He berated the commander of Army Group Center, Fedor von Bock, by telephone and sent Wilhelm Keitel, chief of the armed forces high command, to Bock's headquarters in order to make certain the Smolensk circle was closed. Hoth's 20th Motorized Infantry Division finally sealed it on July 26. Infantry from the Ninth Army, which had lagged behind, undertook the time-consuming work of corralling the trapped enemy. It was August 5 before Bock could announce in his order of the day that the Smolensk pocket had been eliminated, but the results impressed even the Führer: 310,000 prisoners taken, 3,205 tanks and 3,120 guns destroyed or captured.

Guderian, meanwhile, was securing his southern flank by skillfully constructing another encirclement at Roslavl, a rail center sixty-five miles southeast of Smolensk. For this operation—against a Soviet army that had harried his right flank since July 18—Guderian was assigned two additional corps of infantry. He questioned whether these unfamiliar units would perform up to the standards of his regular troops. One of the outfits, the IX Corps, was commanded by Lieut. General Hermann Geyer, a distin-

Shifting Muscle to the Flanks

After Smolensk fell on July 16, the two panzer groups *(dark red)* of Army Group Center failed to quickly close the vice around the Soviet forces north and east of the city. Both spearheads were suffering consequences of the eastward dash, which stretched supply lines and exposed their flanks and rear to counterattack. Pressing on despite these hazards, Hoth's Panzer Group 3 passed Smolensk to the north to cut the Minsk-to-Moscow highway at Yartsevo, thirty miles east. Then Hoth waited to rendezvous with Guderian's Panzer Group 2. But instead of turning north, Guderian sent his armor east to secure the high ground around Yelnya before advancing on Moscow. As a result, tens of thousands of Russians escaped before Hoth finally closed the pocket on July 26. During August, the northern part of Army Group Center's front remained largely static, while Guderian's panzers and the Second Army cleared out the enemy along the southern flank, setting the stage for an encirclement at Kiev.

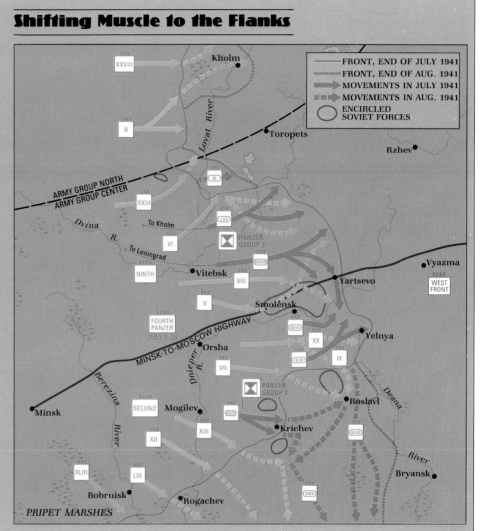

guished veteran of the Great War who had twice served as Guderian's superior. Guderian's suggestion that Geyer's troops were untested in battle affronted his old commander. Geyer pointed out that one division alone, the 137th Infantry, had suffered 2,000 casualties since Barbarossa began.

Meeting with his corps commanders in a Russian schoolhouse, Guderian unveiled a plan for what he considered a textbook encirclement north of Roslavl. One of the infantry corps would attack in a southeasterly direction to tie down the enemy. From the northeast, Geyer's IX Corps would push to the south, turn west across the Russian rear, and meet a panzer division cutting eastward. Geyer thought he detected flaws in Guderian's plan and told him so, but Guderian was unswayed. "I had to put up a stubborn self-defense against the remarks of my old commander," he wrote, "during that conference in the little Russian schoolroom."

Once the attack had begun, Guderian went out of his way to set an example for Geyer's troops. On August 3, the third day of the operation, the advance of the regiment on the extreme left wing slackened. To speed things up, Guderian inserted himself into the lead rifle company and marched for a while with the men. The word raced back through the ranks that "Fast Heinz" was slogging along with the foot soldiers. In this way, Guderian wrote, he "ensured that there were no needless delays, without having to waste many words to do so."

Two days later, when the pocket had nearly been closed, Guderian rushed to a gap northeast of Roslavl that was rapidly filling with Russians. Enraged at this threat to his encirclement, he maneuvered a company of panzers into position, then organized a mixed bag of infantry and artillery and led it into action. An aide saw him shortly thereafter standing next to a hot-barreled machine gun, drinking mineral water from a cup and exclaiming, "Anger gives you a thirst!"

Thanks in no small part to Guderian's anger, the Germans sealed the gap. In a week, Guderian's forces had swiftly and efficiently drawn a noose around the Soviets at Roslavl and captured more than 38,000 prisoners. During the next fortnight, similar encirclements to the southwest, at Krichev and Gomel, took 78,000 additional captives.

During the early days of August, still another battle of encirclement raged 400 miles to the south, around the Ukrainian city of Uman. It had been precipitated by Army Group South's fast-moving panzers, under an old cavalryman, General Ewald von Kleist. His proud men painted a large white letter *K* on their 600 tanks and other vehicles, and at least some of the tankers were unusually well fed: The 16th Panzer Division had captured a Red Army storehouse containing one million eggs, and the division's cooks spent the next weeks devising new ways to serve them.

After Hitler had diverted Kleist's panzers from Kiev, their original objective, in mid-July, the tank columns cut southeast, driving deep into the rear area of Soviet forces falling back to the Dnieper River. The panzers swept past Uman, turned south, and severed the Soviet line of retreat. While the armor formed blocking positions to discourage counterattacks from the east, two German infantry armies converged on Uman to create the remaining arcs of the encirclement. The Sixth Army descended from the northwest and the Seventeenth Army approached from the west (*map, page 65*). At Hitler's behest, the encirclement was to be more compact than the huge Minsk and Smolensk pockets, whose size had made them porous.

Many of the infantry units would have to march 100 miles or more to take positions around Uman. By day, the sun and heat oppressed them; at night, the rain drenched them and turned the dirt tracks that passed for roads into ankle-deep mud. West of Uman, along the Southern Bug River, the Soviets counterattacked in a vigorous attempt to break up bridgeheads established east of the Bug by the XLIX Mountain Corps.

"The Soviet infantry came forward in trucks," reported a German officer, "trying to use mass to smother the defense. Their attacks were made in waves of vehicles in which the infantry stood, firing all the time." Then, wrote the officer, German forward observers called in fire from assault

In the battle-scarred town of Roslavl, General Heinz Guderian (*second from left*), commander of Panzer Group 2, confers with his former superior, Lieut. General Hermann Geyer (*facing camera at right*), commander of the IX Infantry Corps. Their encircling operation trapped more than 38,000 Russian troops.

guns—75-mm howitzers mounted on Panzer III chassis. "I saw one assault gun, firing from a standstill, smash every vehicle of the leading group of about eighteen trucks in less than three minutes. Fire! A direct hit. Fire! A direct hit. Fire! Fire! Fire! And so on."

The fighting grew more intense after August 2, when the first of the German infantry arrived on foot to link up with the panzers southeast of Uman. The ring around the Soviets was now in place, but it had gaps and weak spots. As the Germans tried to strengthen the trap, formations of Soviet infantry and Cossack cavalry, the riders bent low in the saddle, flung themselves repeatedly at the encirclement.

"The speed with which Ivan built up his strength was incredible," re-

At Nikopol, in the Ukraine, General Ewald von Kleist, commander of Panzer Group 1, instructs officers of the Hungarian corps attached to his command. The Hungarians proved more interested in keeping an eye on their longtime enemies, the Rumanians, than in fighting Russians.

called a German. "A pocket of Russians unclear at last light would be a battalion in well-prepared defensive positions at first light the next morning. Then, at the last moment, would come their battle cry, and they would stampede out of the mist, shoulder to shoulder, wave after wave. We shot them down in batches, but there were always more to storm forward."

German patrols probed the pocket at their peril. Mines and camouflaged pits lined with sharp stakes awaited them. Soviet snipers zeroed in from treetops, where they had tied themselves to limbs to free both hands for aiming and firing. Entire Russian units secreted themselves in hollows under the cover of the thick white mist that formed when the daytime heat collided with the cool, rain-soaked ground.

During that fierce first week in August, the German mountain troops along the southern perimeter worked feverishly to beat back the Soviet assaults. The Russians inside the ring threw everything into their last breakout attempt: infantry on foot, then cavalry, and finally tanks, followed by trucks carrying more infantry. They drove a wedge into the sector held by the mountain corps, which suffered heavily, losing 5,000 men in all.

The Russian counterattacks temporarily cut off four guns of the 9th Battery, 94th Mountain Artillery Regiment, from their infantry support. Firing in a frenzy of self-defense—sometimes at such close range they simply blazed away over open sights—the crews turned back repeated Russian attacks. The gunners afterward claimed the destruction of one tank, 16 guns, and 110 trucks. In four days, they had fired 1,150 rounds, more ammunition than the battery had expended during the entire campaign in France the previous year.

The ground around Uman was strewn thick with the dead; a German

Sweeping across the Steppes

As Kleist's Panzer Group 1 closed in on Kiev, Hitler grew impatient with Army Group South's failure to close the noose around the retreating Russian armies. To remedy this, he ordered Panzer Group 1 to veer southeastward away from Kiev and cut behind the enemy forces being driven back to the Dnieper by the Sixth, Seventeenth, and Eleventh Armies pushing in from the west. The Russians guessed the Germans' intentions and fought hard to stave off encirclement. But on August 2, lead elements of Panzer Group 1 captured Pervomaysk and effectively cut off some twenty Soviet divisions concentrated around Uman. Then the infantry closed in, crushing the last resistance six days later. The victory freed Army Group South to overrun all of the western Ukraine and push on across the Dnieper.

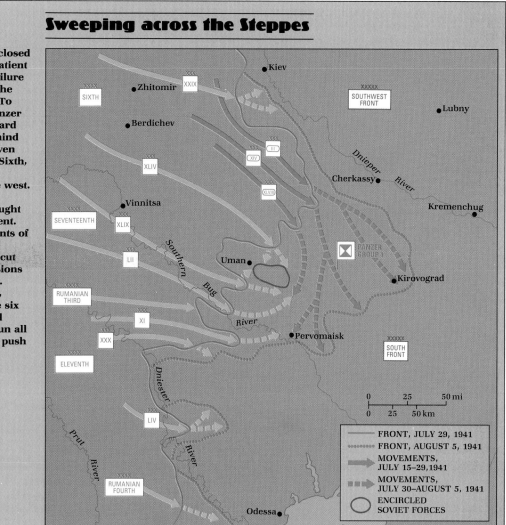

remembered it as "one huge grave-yard." Another German recalled the burned-out Soviet trucks: "In some, there would be whole rows of Russian soldiers sitting on the floor of the vehicles and burned to cinders. The drivers still sat, blackened to charcoal, at the wheels of the trucks, and the terrible smell of bodies burning was everywhere, a stink that even overrode that of burning rubber from the tires."

Most of all, the Uman battlefield—like those in the other encirclements—became during the second week in August an enormous corral for gathering up captives. The war diary of the XLIX Mountain Corps reported, "The prisoners march in an unbroken column, eight abreast, and the column stretches across the rolling countryside for more than ten kilometers." The 103,000 prisoners of war taken at Uman, like the 800,000 other Russians already in German captivity, faced a bleak future of extreme deprivation. Even before surrendering, many of them had been cut off from their food supplies and were nearly starved. They were too weak to survive the long march to the rear. Their German captors had not anticipated such prodigious harvests of prisoners and were unprepared to feed and care for them.

Those captives strong enough to escape and return to their own lines found themselves forsaken by their government. The Soviet regime considered surrender a sign of political unreliability. A prisoner of war who made it back was treated not as a hero but as a traitor to be shot or sent to Siberia. To further discourage surrender, the law permitted the jailing of a prisoner's relatives. After Stalin's eldest son Yakov, an artillery officer, had surrendered in the Smolensk pocket, the Soviet dictator disowned him and imprisoned Yakov's wife.

A machine-gun crew of the German 1st Mountain Division supports an attack across a stubbly field aimed at reducing Soviet resistance around Uman. The elite alpine troops felt their talents were being wasted on the flat Ukrainian steppes.

A German assault gun *(foreground)* leads a column of motorized infantry in the maneuvering to encircle Uman. Assault guns spearheading infantry attacks suffered heavy losses; their crews were said to enjoy "short but eventful lives."

At the end of August, three weeks after the battle of Uman, Adolf Hitler encountered his first Russian prisoners. He flew to Uman in the company of Benito Mussolini, who reviewed an Italian division that had recently joined Army Group South. Hitler had lunch with the troops, then drove to an old brickyard that bulged with an estimated 74,000 prisoners. The Führer inspected a corner of the camp that had been spruced up for his visit and talked with one of the prisoners, a Red Army physician. The experience seems not to have impressed the Führer nearly as much as the flight home, during which Mussolini, a sometime aviator, insisted on taking the controls of Hitler's aircraft.

On the extreme left of the German invasion force, armored spearheads of Army Group North reached the Luga River in mid-July, after an advance of nearly 400 miles. Leningrad lay only 70 miles to the northeast, but Hitler ordered the panzers to halt at the Luga. He wanted to consolidate his gains before launching a final offensive against Russia's longtime imperial capital. To the left of Erich Hoepner's Panzer Group 4, the Eighteenth Army needed time to clear remnants of the Red Army from the Baltic states of Estonia and Latvia. On the right, the Sixteenth Army still struggled to catch up with Hoepner's panzers and maintain contact with the left flank of Army Group Center.

From the beginning, the terrain in the north had frustrated the German advance. The panzers had encountered a landscape laced with rivers, lakes, and marshes; expanses of loose sand alternated with dense forests. As a result, the German tanks had been unable to execute the daring breakthroughs, encirclements, and pincer movements that had netted huge catches of Russian prisoners elsewhere on the front. Conditions

worsened as the approaches to Leningrad narrowed between two lakes, Peipus and Ilmen. The city itself, situated on the thirty-mile-wide Karelian Isthmus between the Gulf of Finland and Lake Ladoga, was built in low-lying marshes on more than 100 islands.

In the sector on the right held by the LVI Panzer Corps, even tracked vehicles bogged down amid the muck and other obstacles. Uncharted bodies of water appeared; bridges collapsed without warning under the weight of the panzers. By the time a halt was called on the Luga, the terrain had utterly frustrated the corps's commander, Erich von Manstein, who suggested pulling all of his panzers out of the north and shifting them to the center for use against Moscow.

Manstein's distaste for Hitler's tactics may have prompted the suggestion. The German armor was dispersed along the Luga River on a front nearly seventy-five miles long. Manstein's corps stood near the town of Luga, and Georg-Hans Reinhardt's XLI Corps was closer to the Baltic Sea, near Narva (map, page 73). Both Manstein and Reinhardt advocated concentration, one of the basic tenets of blitzkrieg; they wanted to put all the panzers on the left, near Narva, where the roads were better and the Red Army defenses weaker. They remembered all too well that Manstein's panzers had been temporarily cut off from their supply line in mid-July because of orders deploying them too far to the right, on marshy ground. But Hitler insisted on outflanking Leningrad from the right, or southeast, rather than from the left, in order to trap more of the retreating enemy.

The good news for Manstein and the other commanders on the northern front was that, despite the confusion and vacillation at Wolfsschanze, Hitler had lost none of his appetite for seizing Leningrad. He considered the city vitally important—both strategically, as the base of the Soviet Baltic Fleet, and politically, as the place from which Lenin had launched the Bolshevik Revolution. Late in July, the Führer visited the headquarters of Wilhelm Ritter von Leeb, commander of Army Group North, and promised reinforcements for the final assault against Leningrad: substantial numbers of planes and panzers from Army Group Center, as well as help from the Finns, who would seal off the city from the north and east.

The German advance on Leningrad resumed on August 8. On the left, Reinhardt's XLI Panzer Corps broke out of its bridgeheads but immediately ran into determined resistance. The Red Army had made use of the three-week lull on the lower Luga to build field fortifications and bring in reinforcements, some of whom disembarked from the railroad in full view of the Germans. Strengthened, the Russians inflicted severe casualties on the first day of the German attack. Reinhardt seriously considered suspending his offensive, but the next day brought renewed German effort. One of

Reinhardt's panzer divisions penetrated the Luga line and raced thirty miles ahead, while other units pushed through the breach and followed.

By August 15, the road to Leningrad had been cleared for Reinhardt's spearhead. The hulks of dozens of brand-new Soviet KV tanks, some of which had been crewed by women and civilian inspectors from the factory, littered the battlefield. The only threat to Reinhardt's panzers now lay on his left flank, where Soviet forces were falling back toward Leningrad from Estonia. To protect that flank, Leeb agreed to shift a motorized division from Manstein's panzer corps, which had stalled near the town of Luga.

It was not surprising that Manstein's attack had fizzled—he had neither tanks nor much of anything else. His crack 8th Panzer Division unaccountably had been detached and sent to clear out partisans operating in the rear—"a role," Manstein wrote later, "for which it was not only far too valuable but also quite unsuitable." One of the corps's two motorized infantry units, the SS Totenkopf, or Death's-Head, Division, had been assigned to support the Sixteenth Army. Now the other mobile unit, the 3d Motorized Infantry Division, was on its way to help Reinhardt, and Manstein was left to attack the Luga line with only two regular infantry divisions. Stripped of his striking power, Manstein made little headway. The baton was passed to Reinhardt, who raced northeastward toward his goal.

Just when the capture of Leningrad seemed imminent, a perilous new crisis flared on the far right flank of Army Group North. Attacking from the southeast, a Soviet army with eight infantry divisions abetted by cavalry and armor stormed into the widening funnel created by the diverging paths of Army Groups North and Center. In the area south of Lake Ilmen, this Soviet force slammed into the right flank of the Sixteenth Army's X Corps, which had just overrun Staraya Russa, and pushed on to the Lovat River. Although the Soviet attack occurred more than 150 miles southeast of Reinhardt's spearhead, the Russian commander on this front, Marshal Kliment Voroshilov, hoped nevertheless to cripple the advance on Leningrad. He intended to smash the three divisions of the X Corps, then drive west and sever the supply lines of the panzers.

The Soviet gambit prompted the Germans to dispatch northward the long-promised help from Army Group Center—the XXXIX Panzer Corps of Hoth's Panzer Group 3. But the only immediate hope for blocking Voroshilov was Manstein's dispersed panzer corps, which was ordered to the rescue late on August 15. The next day, Manstein raced southeast toward the action with only his headquarters group. The rest of the corps, however, pulled itself together on the run: The 3d Motorized turned around and headed southeast, and the SS division hurried toward the breach.

As his corps reassembled, Manstein prepared to pay back the Soviets for

German artillerymen ride through the burning city of Kingisepp during the August advance on Leningrad. The invading army relied on old-fashioned horse power for 80 percent of its transport.

their surprise flank attack. Over the next two days, he maneuvered his units eastward without being detected. Early on August 19, as the Russians faced north, threatening to drive the three infantry divisions of the X Corps into Lake Ilmen, he struck the enemy's exposed left flank. The sudden onslaught panicked the Soviet troops. Attacked from the west by Manstein and counterattacked from the north by the X Corps, the Russian formations crumbled. Over the next three days, Manstein's motorized infantry drove the Soviets eastward across the Lovat River, pursuing them much of the way on foot because the sandy roads were too soft for trucks.

Manstein's brilliant thrust netted 12,000 prisoners, 141 tanks, and the first Katyusha rocket launcher to fall into German hands. "As I was most anxious to have the latter evacuated," Manstein wrote, "I was all the more indignant to find that it could not be moved because somebody had helped himself to the tires! The offender proved to be none other than my aide, Major Niemann, who had discovered that these tires fit our own command trailer. He looked somewhat crestfallen when told to hand them back for reassembly." Manstein had to content himself with his unusual booty and the honor of thwarting Voroshilov's bold move, because he would not rejoin Reinhardt's panzer assault on Leningrad. Almost immediately, Voroshilov moved three new armies into position on the Lovat River, and Manstein's corps had to remain, along with two corps of infantry, to disrupt any fresh Soviet initiative.

To the north, meanwhile, beyond the far shore of Lake Ilmen, elements of the German Sixteenth Army fought to cut a vital communications link to Leningrad. The operation began when the I Corps, led by the 21st Infantry Division, skirted the western shore of the lake and advanced on the historic city of Novgorod, established in the ninth century. Novgorod was heavily fortified, but the Germans seized it quickly after receiving some fortuitous help from the enemy: A disaffected Red Army officer, captured by a reconnaissance detachment of the 45th Infantry Regiment, provided maps of the city's strongpoints and minefields.

From Novgorod, the German infantry marched north along the Volkhov River forty-five miles to the key railroad junction of Chudovo. Not only was this city an important stop on the railway between Moscow and Leningrad, it was also the southern terminus of the line descending from Murmansk, the ice-free port on the Arctic Sea where tanks, ammunition, and other matériel from the United States and Britain would soon start arriving. At the Chudovo junction, trains laden with arms and supplies could be switched to Leningrad, sixty miles to the northwest, or sent to the southeast for deployment along the entire Soviet front. On August 20, German infantrymen seized the road and rail bridges over the Volkhov River south of Chudovo and, five days later, took the town itself.

Hitler wanted to encircle Leningrad, then level it. In Halder's words, the Führer wanted to render that lovely city "uninhabitable so as to relieve us of the necessity of having to feed the population through the winter." Hitler considered the city a "poisonous nest" that "must vanish from the earth's surface." The encirclement he sought took shape slowly during the last days of August and the first week of September. The German infantry advanced from the southeast; from the southwest, Reinhardt's panzers moved cautiously to within twenty miles of the city's outskirts. Infantry of the Eighteenth Army, which had finally completed the task of ousting Soviet troops from Estonia, moved up on Reinhardt's left flank.

The Surge North to Leningrad

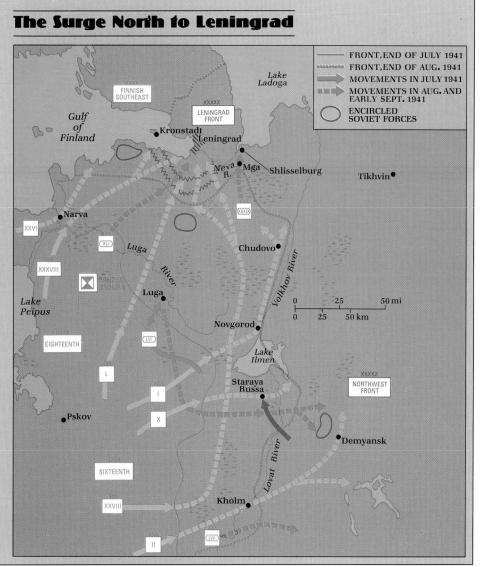

By mid-July, Reinhardt's XLI Panzer Corps had reached the Luga, seventy miles southwest of Leningrad, and the city's fall seemed imminent. But to take more prisoners, Hitler wanted the main attack on the right. For three weeks, Reinhardt stood while the rest of Army Group North struggled forward and the panzer commanders argued in vain to concentrate their armor on the left. On August 8, the Germans finally struck. A defensive line thrown up during the lull halted Reinhardt's corps, but the next morning the defenders broke and the Germans raced toward the city. Manstein's LVI Panzer Corps bogged down on the right because it had been stripped of its mobile units. On August 15, Manstein got back two divisions. At Lake Ilmen, he smashed an attack against the flank of the Sixteenth Army. Meanwhile, the bulk of Army Group North was nearing Leningrad—Reinhardt's corps and the Eighteenth Army from the southwest, and the Sixteenth Army from the southeast. During the second week of September, they hammered into the city's defensive perimeter and cut its last overland link with the outside.

The narrow northern approach to Leningrad, meanwhile, was sealed off courtesy of the army of Finland. During July, the Finns had attacked on both sides of Lake Ladoga and advanced rapidly. To Hitler's consternation, however, the Finns halted and switched to the defensive as soon as they regained the territory lost to the Soviet Union during the Winter War. Although the Finnish troops on the Karelian Isthmus had dug in less than thirty miles from the northern fringes of Leningrad, they would go no farther than their old frontier despite German pressure and entreaties.

On September 4, German long-range artillery began pumping shells into the outskirts of the city, the first of 30,154 rounds that would be directed there before the end of the year. On the night of September 6, the Luftwaffe's bombers joined the attack. They returned two nights later to drop thousands of incendiaries, which set fire to the Badayev warehouses, a four-acre complex of wooden buildings that held much of the city's food supply. The flour and fats burned furiously, lighting the sky for successive waves of German bombers. Leningrad's entire reserves of sugar—2,500 tons— melted and ran into neighboring cellars, where it solidified like hard candy.

The Luftwaffe dominated the skies over Leningrad. When Soviet General Georgy Zhukov arrived by air to take command of the city's defense, a pair

of Messerschmitt fighters dogged his plane as it descended. Zhukov, who as chief of the general staff had developed the overall Soviet defensive strategy, had been dismissed by Stalin in July in a dispute over how best to defend the Ukraine. Now Stalin had dispatched him to save Leningrad.

Zhukov found a city under siege. A workers' militia armed with shotguns and Molotov cocktails—gasoline-filled bottles with wicks—had mobilized to supplement the nearly forty divisions of regulars in and around the city. Men, women, and children from Leningrad's population of three million worked to complete two concentric arcs of bunkers, antitank ditches, and other fortifications covering the southern approaches to the city.

On September 8 and 9, the Germans attacked these fortifications on a broad front. In the center, motorized infantry led an assault by Reinhardt's XLI Panzer Corps. Supported by screaming Stukas, the infantrymen fought on foot through the outer defensive line twenty-five miles from the center of Leningrad, firing from the hip, hurling grenades, and flicking fiery tongues from their flame throwers into the slits of the enemy pillboxes.

Early on September 10, the assault battalions came up against the formidable inner line of defenses only fifteen miles from the city's center. Anchoring this line were the Duderhof Hills, the historic heights from which the czars had watched the maneuvers of their guards regiments. The Germans paid for every yard of progress against the web of concrete pillboxes, interconnecting trenches, and casemates bristling with big naval guns—defenses further strengthened by Soviet heavy KV-1 and KV-2 tanks, so fresh from the factory they lacked a full coat of paint.

Above, smoke from the industrial district of Leningrad obscures the dome of Saint Isaac Cathedral following a raid by the Luftwaffe. At right, crew members of a German coastal battery cover their ears as they launch a mortar shell toward the Soviet island fortress of Kronstadt.

A crisis developed on the right of the attacking German columns. The 6th Panzer Division forged too far ahead and was hit in the flank by a Russian counterattack. Within the next few hours, the division suffered heavy casualties, including four successive commanding officers. Reinhardt moved up the 1st Panzer Division to buttress the 6th, and before dark, German infantry successfully stormed one of the two commanding heights in the Duderhof ridge, Hill 143. To the east of the hill, tanks from the 1st Panzer took positions in front of the German line and beat back Soviet counterattacks through a night illuminated by the ghoulish light of sodium flares and blazing gasoline.

At dawn on September 11, the 1st Panzer set out to capture the other key height in the enemy's defense network. This was Hill 167, known to the Germans as Bald Hill because of its sparse cover. The division's motorized infantry, traveling in armored personnel carriers, led the way. A platoon of sappers bridged a deep antitank ditch with beams and planks, and the troop carriers and panzers raced forward. Luftwaffe liaison officers rode with them and radioed targets to the Stukas striking from above. When the Soviet naval guns on the hillside began to thunder, German sappers worked up to the emplacements under covering fire from the panzers and cleaned out the enemy crews in hand-to-hand fighting.

At half past eleven that morning, division headquarters overheard the radio signal it was waiting for. Members of the staff cheered, and also chuckled, at the romanticism of the message, sent from a young tank officer on Bald Hill to his battalion commander: "I can see St. Petersburg and the sea," he reported, referring to the city by its former name. Downtown Leningrad was less than fifteen miles away, almost at the feet of the awe-struck lieutenant, who stood on the crest of Hill 167 and stared down at the historic spires and domes.

Three days earlier, the Germans had taken another important objective east of Leningrad. The town of Shlisselburg stood sentinel on the southwestern corner of Lake Ladoga, where the Neva River begins its twenty-five-mile journey westward to Leningrad and the Baltic Sea. On this site 239 years earlier, Peter the Great had fought the battle against the Swedes that won the Russians access to the Baltic. To protect that access, he founded St. Petersburg. Shlisselburg, meanwhile, had lived up to its name, "key fortress": It guarded the waterway between Lake Ladoga and the Gulf of Finland and the eastern approaches to Leningrad's narrow isthmus.

Shlisselburg fell on September 8 to the 20th Motorized Infantry Division, part of the XXXIX Panzer Corps, which had recently been transferred from Army Group Center. The town's capture completed the sealing off of Leningrad. Now the city's only connection to the rest of the Soviet Union—its lifeline, in the fullest sense—ran northeastward, across the isthmus and thence across the lake. Leningrad was ripe for the plucking.

As Hitler's northern armies closed on Leningrad, he vacillated about priorities farther south. What Manstein later characterized as "all this chopping and changing" was provoked by pressure from the Wehrmacht's leading generals and perhaps also by illness. Hitler suffered from the dysentery that was common in the swampy surroundings of his East Prussian headquarters, and his weakened physical state may help explain the indecision that influenced developments on the battlefields.

It was clear by late July that the German army lacked the men and matériel to pursue objectives in the north, south, and center simultaneously. Enemy action, the long distances covered, and the incessant dust strained the panzers of Army Group Center more each day. The grit-clogged engines were using twice as much oil as usual and wearing out much faster than anticipated. By early August, Guderian was begging for replacements. His panzer group had begun the invasion with nearly 1,000 tanks; now scarcely one in four was still battleworthy. Hitler had not a single new tank to offer. Instead, he promised to send 300 new tank engines, but that allotment would have to satisfy the entire front.

Merely getting the engines and other supplies to the front presented a challenge. Railways in captured Soviet territory were being converted to the narrower European gauge slowly, so most of the armies' requirements had to come by truck over great distances—more than 400 miles in the center. About one truck in three never made it, falling prey instead to mechanical breakdowns or ambushes by the bands of Soviet partisans and Red Army stragglers that increasingly threatened the German rear.

Replacements for battlefield casualties were also falling short. By late August, after ten weeks of combat, German losses totaled 440,000 men, and only about half that number were arriving to take their place. As the invasion force shrank, the Red Army expanded—despite casualties of nearly two million, nearly half of whom were prisoners. The Russians had the luxury of tapping 5.3 million reservists, who had been mobilized shortly after the invasion of their homeland. "At the outset of the war, we reckoned with about 200 enemy divisions," Halder wrote with obvious frustration in his diary on August 11. "Now we have already counted 360. If we smash a dozen of them, the Russians simply put up another dozen."

Halder was still pressing the Führer to renew the drive in the center. On August 18, he and his superior, the army commander in chief, Walther von Brauchitsch, wrote Hitler, strongly urging him to resume the march on Moscow. On August 21, Hitler replied to his recalcitrant commanders. He ordered Army Group Center, which had already sent two panzer corps

Soldiers of the 126th Infantry Division patrol the Neva River in Shlisselburg, a city on Lake Ladoga, twenty-five miles east of Leningrad. By capturing Shlisselburg, the Germans cut the last land route between Leningrad and the rest of the Soviet Union.

north, now to dispatch forces south to expedite the conquest of the Ukraine. The first objective would be the city of Kiev, which Hitler had forbidden his panzers to occupy back in July. If all this were not exasperating enough for Halder and Brauchitsch, a few hours later the Führer sent them a memorandum bristling with references to unnamed commanders who were driven by "selfish desires" and whose minds were "fossilized in out-of-date theories." Halder, outraged, suggested that they both resign, but Brauchitsch refused, contending that "it wouldn't be practical and would change nothing."

In a last-ditch effort to resurrect the Moscow plan, Halder flew to the headquarters of Army Group Center near Minsk on August 23. He suggested that one of the assembled commanders should go to the Führer and, speaking as a general fresh from the battlefield, make a final plea for the advance on Moscow. The obvious choice was Guderian. The outspoken panzer leader was one of Hitler's favorite generals despite his tendency to argue about strategy and a streak of arrogance that occasionally led him to disobey orders. A proponent of the Moscow strategy, he had ordered his staff to prepare for an advance on the Soviet capital even after Hitler had rejected it as the prime target. He took every opportunity to lobby for the cause, even badgering the Führer's adjutant when he arrived to decorate Guderian with the oak leaves to the Knight's Cross, an award that only four others in the German army had received. Guderian, who was fiercely protective of his command, now had an even greater stake in the Moscow strategy. Hitler's new plan called for Guderian's Panzer Group 2 to be split: Part was to head to the Ukraine, the rest to remain in the center. The panzer general intended to keep his command intact.

Halder wasted no time in scheduling Guderian for an audience with Hitler. The general flew immediately to Wolfsschanze, where he was received warmly that same evening. Hitler listened patiently while Guderian made the now-familiar case that "the fall of Moscow will decide the war." Guderian argued that the 250-mile diversion to Kiev would be too much for his worn-out panzers and might make it impossible later to reverse direction and capture Moscow before the winter. Hitler then rose and lectured Guderian on the economic benefits of conquering the Ukraine. "My generals," scolded the Führer, "know nothing about the economic aspects of war." Guderian, having failed to convince the Führer, decided to salvage what he could from their conference. "I begged Hitler not to split my panzer group, as was intended, but to commit the whole group to the operation. Thus a rapid victory might be won before the autumn rains came. This request was granted."

The outcome bitterly disappointed Halder. He had secretly hoped to

German infantry combat dress (*shown front and rear*) consisted of a model 1935 steel helmet, field blouse, and trousers. The model 1935 tunic kept the dark green collar and insignia backing of peacetime dress. The soldier fastened a spade and gas mask (*bottom*) at his left hip.

Battle Kit for the Footsloggers

"The infantry pays the highest price," griped a German private. "When we're not fighting, we march, sometimes forty miles a day, along the deeply rutted roads, through patches of loose sand and clouds of dust, heading always eastward." Those unsung pedestrians—117 divisions strong—formed the sturdy backbone of Adolf Hitler's crusade against bolshevist Russia. Unlike their comrades in the mechanized forces, the two million *Landsers*, or footsloggers, lugged all of their equipment—combat gear, weapons, tools, and extra clothing—on their persons.

With only a few exceptions, such as a camouflage shelter quarter and an improved gas mask, the German infantryman's equipment had altered little since the turn of the century. He still wore traditional calf-high jackboots and fought with a modified 1898 rifle.

The German soldier of 1941 bore more than fifty pounds of gear, on top of which might be added rations, reserve ammunition, and components for machine guns and mortars. Soldiers on the march soon discarded extraneous or unwanted items, such as mess-kit covers, barracks shoes, and greatcoats, or left them in regimental transport. Instead, their packs, pockets, and bread bags bulged with the small necessities and comforts displayed on the following pages.

Esbit folding stove and box

Fuel tablets

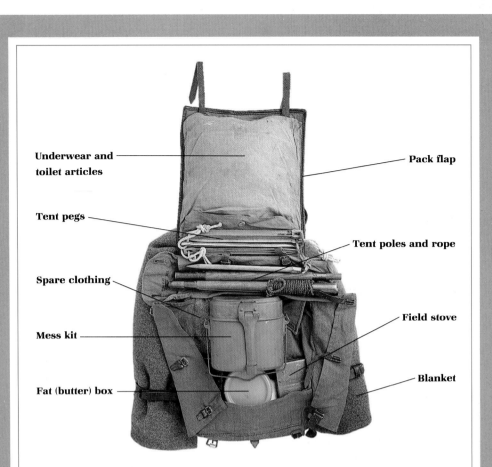

Underwear and toilet articles

Tent pegs

Spare clothing

Mess kit

Fat (butter) box

Pack flap

Tent poles and rope

Field stove

Blanket

In the field, the *Landser* lived out of a canvas-and-leather pack (*above*), in which he carried his personal gear and extra clothing. Prewar regulations defined how the pack's contents should be arranged, but as the items on these pages show, soldiers were allowed leeway in suiting the load to the conditions they faced.

They strapped either a greatcoat or a blanket to the outside of the pack, along with such special equipment as the company's ax or shovel. Because their pack's rigid wooden frame limited the amount that could be stuffed inside, more and more foot soldiers shouldered expandable rucksacks as the war went on.

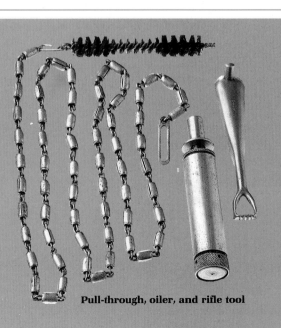

Spoon and fork

Hindenburg candle

Muzzle cover

Rifle-cleaning kit

Pull-through, oiler, and rifle tool

Chocolate candy

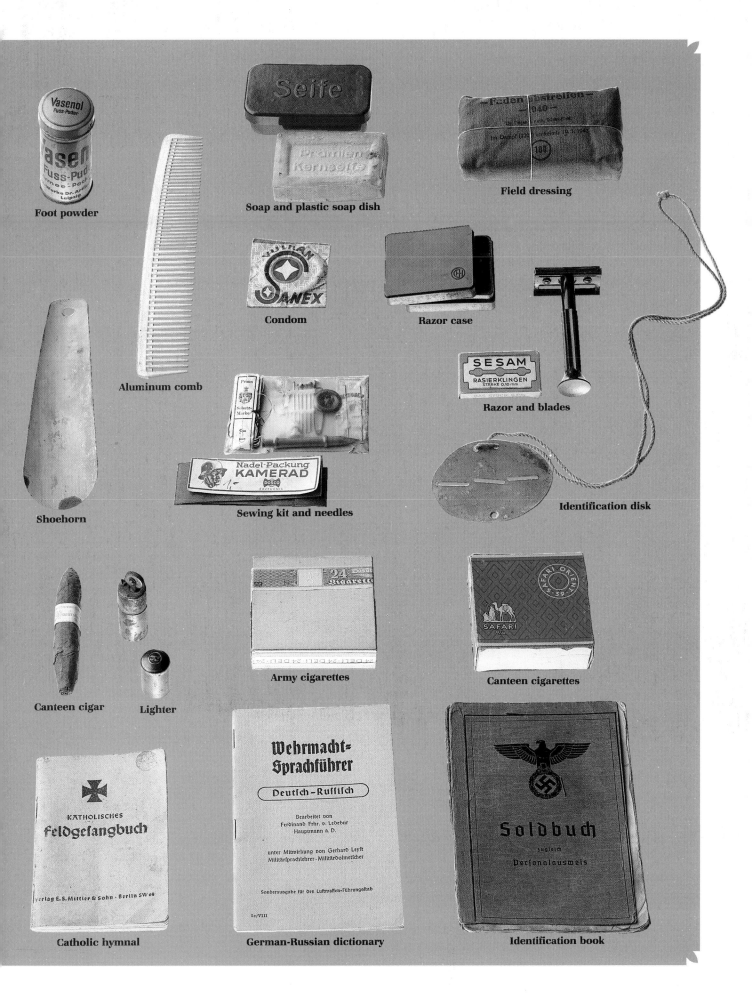

Foot powder

Soap and plastic soap dish

Field dressing

Condom

Razor case

Aluminum comb

Razor and blades

Shoehorn

Sewing kit and needles

Identification disk

Canteen cigar

Lighter

Army cigarettes

Canteen cigarettes

Catholic hymnal

German-Russian dictionary

Identification book

hold back part of Guderian's panzers and husband them for the eventual drive on Moscow. He considered Hitler's agreement to keep Panzer Group 2 intact nothing but a bribe to entice Guderian to cooperate with the Kiev operation. Halder accused the panzer leader of betrayal. "To my amazement," Guderian wrote, "he suffered a complete nervous collapse, which led him to make accusations and imputations that were utterly unjustified." If Halder's plan had backfired, however, he later won a small victory by contriving to withhold Guderian's XLVI Panzer Corps in reserve near Smolensk while the rest of the group turned south toward Kiev.

For the new operation in the heart of the Ukraine, the Germans planned to entrap one million Soviet troops in another enormous encirclement, this time around Kiev. A small part of Army Group South—the Eleventh Army, along with its Rumanian allies—would be assigned the separate mission

After the triumph at Roslavl, armored personnel carriers of Guderian's Panzer Group 2 roll southward to join in the encirclement of Kiev. Because of its mobility and firepower, the motorized infantry came to be known as the Wehrmacht's secret weapon.

of advancing southeast toward the Black Sea and the Crimea, but all the rest would join the envelopment. The Sixth Army was to push toward Kiev from the west. Strong forces already southeast of the city—Kleist's Panzer Group 1, supported by the Seventeenth Army—would drive north. This pincer would be met by the force driving south from Army Group Center—two corps of Guderian's Panzer Group 2, accompanied on their right by elements of the Second Army (map, page 85).

Guderian started south on August 25, a blistering summer day. Clouds of dust settled upon the vehicles, which were emblazoned with a big white letter G. Previous operations to secure the German flank south of Smolensk had already taken his spearheads nearly half the distance to their destination east of Kiev. The lead tanks of the 3d Panzer Division covered nearly sixty miles that day, and at nightfall they approached their first objective: the Desna River at Novgorod-Severski, about 150 miles northeast of Kiev. The river here was more than 600 yards wide and ran between steep, clifflike banks 300 yards high. To cross it, the Germans would have to prevent the defenders from blowing up a 750-yard-long wooden bridge.

Early the next morning, the energetic and resourceful division commander, Major General Walter Model, dispatched a small combat group toward the town and the river. The force included a detachment of tanks from the 6th Panzer Regiment and a column of armored infantry carriers bearing sappers under the command of a lieutenant named Störck. Soon after the attack unit moved out, a loud explosion from the direction of a pedestrian bridge across the Desna indicated that the Russians had begun demolition. The sappers raced ahead into Novgorod-Severski, blending into columns of retreating Russian vehicles under a cover of thick dust, and quickly worked their way to the river. They found the main bridge still standing. Five of the Germans overcame the Russian guards and ran onto the span, where wires to demolition charges had been attached to the railings. The men ripped out the wires and pushed the charges into the river. In the center of the bridge lay a Russian aerial bomb, its time fuze ticking. Störck examined the mechanism and then, with icy calm, unscrewed the detonator. The sappers then heaved the disarmed bomb out of the way and ran to the far shore. They fired a flare to signal all clear to the task force of panzers waiting on the western bank.

Russian officers on the east bank also saw the flare and sent demolition squads to the bridge. The engineers hurried beneath the bridge footing and climbed onto the beams with cans of gasoline, Molotov cocktails, and explosive charges. A surprise awaited them. While most of the German panzers had been providing cover from atop the west bank, a single tank, commanded by a Lieutenant Buchterkirch, had driven down the bank and

General Mikhail Kirponos *(right)*, commander of the Soviet defenses at Kiev, strolls with a fellow officer before the German siege began. Kirponos was killed on September 20, when he and his staff attempted to break out of the encirclement.

stopped under the bridge to guard against any attempt to blow it up. Buchterkirch was in perfect position, and his machine gunner mowed down the Soviet demolition squads. Because of his foresight and the quickness of the sappers, Model's armored spearheads were rolling across the bridge within the hour.

Guderian moved with haste to broaden and deepen the bridgehead across the Desna. A division of panzers and one of motorized infantry crossed at Novgorod-Severski to reinforce Model's 3d Panzer, but Russian resistance stiffened. Fifteen miles downstream, the 10th Motorized Division was rudely tossed back from its toehold on the east bank. A catastrophe was averted, Guderian wrote, only "by sending in the very last men of the division, in this case the field bakery company."

Intense fighting that Guderian referred to as a "bloody boxing match" raged for a week on the ground just beyond the Desna. During this period,

The Enormous Trap at Kiev

During the last weeks of August, Hitler finalized orders, dreaded by many generals, that would deflect the panzers of Army Group Center from Moscow. On August 23, Guderian's Panzer Group 2, supported on its right by the Second Army, was directed to continue south into the Ukraine, where it would link up with Kleist's armor and trap the Russian armies around Kiev. Expecting Guderian to turn east, the Soviets could only contest river crossings and harass his left flank as the panzer group rolled south. Guderian took Romny on September 10. Two days later, Kleist's Panzer Group 1 broke out of its bridgehead at Kremenchug, on the Dnieper, and raced north. As the spearheads sped to a rendezvous east of Kiev, the Sixth Army pinned down the Russian forces from the west, and the Second Army fell on them from the north. On September 14, Guderian and Kleist met near Lokhvitsa, closing the trap on more than half a million enemy soldiers.

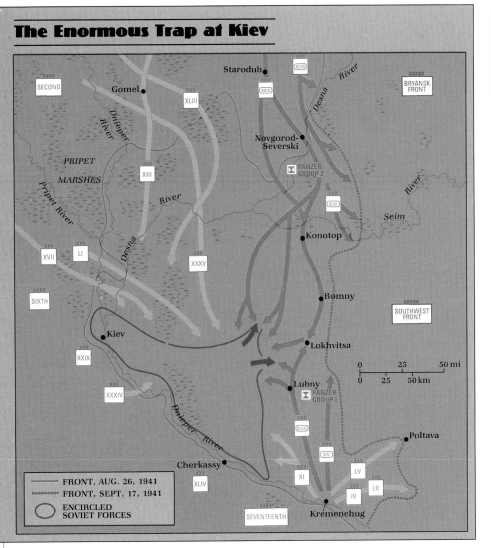

the panzer leader also fought a verbal duel with his superiors in an attempt to retrieve the corps that Halder had kept back. Guderian bombarded both Halder and Bock, the army group commander, with pleas for the return of the XLVI Panzer Corps to bolster his embattled salient at the Desna.

Bock by now was fed up with Guderian's incessant entreaties and protests and wanted to fire him. Halder, however, refused to hear of it, although he was still irritated that Guderian had agreed to join Hitler's campaign in the Ukraine. Halder wrote to a subordinate, "Guderian agreed to this mission, now let him carry it out." Eventually, at the end of August, Halder and Bock began slowly releasing some of Guderian's units in what Guderian sarcastically labeled the "drop-by-drop method of reinforcement."

Assured now of receiving about half of his missing corps, Guderian on September 3 enjoyed another bit of good fortune. A map taken from a downed Soviet aircraft revealed a weak link between two of the Russian armies facing his men. Model's panzers found the gap and broke out of the bridgehead the following morning. After eight days of stalemate on the Desna, Guderian's panzers thrust forward again. On September 7, they crossed the Seim River. Three days later, they occupied the village of Romny, 100 miles east of Kiev and well in the rear of the enemy troops concentrated around the Ukrainian capital.

The trap was ready to spring shut. Some 120 miles to the south, the other

pincer, Kleist's Panzer Group 1, was preparing its thrust northward to meet Guderian. On September 12, Kleist's armor broke out of the bridgehead established by the Seventeenth Army at Kremenchug, on the north bank of the Dnieper River. Fighting through enemy defenders and what Guderian called "canals of mud," Kleist's divisions fanned out across the rolling steppe and raced north, covering more than forty miles on the first day.

Stalin, tracking the latest movements of his enemy, miscalculated on two counts. At first, he had been certain that Guderian, in maneuvering southward, was bound not for Kiev but for Moscow and was simply trying to outflank the Soviet forces deployed before the capital. Then, on September 13, when it became clear that the German jaws were about to close around Kiev, Stalin refused to give local commanders permission to withdraw. "Not a step back," he declared. "Hold out and, if necessary, die."

Smoldering rubble and the bodies of dead soldiers testify to the destruction wrought at Kiev. By the time the shooting stopped on September 26, almost a million Russians had been killed, wounded, or captured in a losing fight for the Ukrainian capital.

In line with the defensive strategy originally developed by Zhukov, Stalin was gambling with men's lives. He was prepared to sacrifice some troops wholesale to buy time to complete the deployment of his strategic reserve around Moscow. On this occasion, however, even Zhukov had balked. Weeks earlier, he had urged the abandonment of Kiev, predicting that losses there would be intolerable and provoking Stalin to dismiss him as chief of the general staff. Now, as Zhukov tried to patch the tattered Soviet position at Leningrad, thousands of Red Army soldiers around Kiev also balked; in disorganized columns they streamed east, seeking gaps among the German mobile formations converging in their rear.

For most of them, it was too late. Shortly after six o'clock in the evening on September 14, a combat group from Model's 3d Panzer Division linked up with an engineer detachment from one of Kleist's divisions near the village of Lokhvitsa, the units having been guided to their rendezvous by a German reconnaissance plane. Model's contingent consisted of only ten tanks—six of them light Panzer II models. They were all that remained of the 6th Panzer Regiment's normal complement of more than 150 tanks; the rest had bogged down in the mud, suffered mechanical failure, or been destroyed by the enemy in the hard fighting that preceded this fateful linkup near a Ukrainian schoolhouse.

The encirclement at Kiev was unprecedented in the history of warfare. Before it began contracting on the Soviet armies confined inside, the ring covered a diameter of some 130 miles. By the time Moscow belatedly authorized withdrawal on September 18, four days after the panzer linkup, the pocket had already degenerated into a cauldron of confusion and killing. The encircled Soviet units tried frantically to find a way out, "ricocheting like billiard balls within the ring," Halder wrote in his diary. Kiev fell on September 19 to infantry of the Sixth Army, even as Stalin's tape-recorded plea to fight to the death bellowed from loudspeakers strung from the trees. The following day, the Soviet commander, General Mikhail Kirponos, heeded the message and died trying to escape the trap.

A week later, Soviet resistance around Kiev collapsed. Never in a single battle had an army suffered a larger defeat. In the month-long campaign against Kiev, the Germans claimed the capture of 884 tanks and other armored vehicles, 3,718 artillery pieces, and the breathtaking total of 665,212 prisoners. All told, the Red Army had lost nearly one million men—dead, wounded, captured, or unaccounted for.

Hitler labeled Kiev "history's greatest battle," but Guderian's weary panzer crews had no time to savor their victory. Almost at once, they regrouped for a new mission, code-named Operation Typhoon. Back on September 6, while the outcome at Kiev was still in doubt, Hitler had changed his mind again and ordered the revival of the long-delayed offensive against Moscow. The need to capture the capital before the onset of the dreaded Russian winter meant there would be no rest for men or machines and insufficient replacements for the German invasion force, whose casualties exceeded 16 percent by the end of September.

After two months of vacillation by Hitler and his high command, the war on the far-flung flanks had suddenly become secondary. From Kiev, Army Group South would push on alone to invade the Crimea and the Donets industrial region. Army Group North would give up most of its panzers to Army Group Center, leaving the siege of Leningrad to the infantry "until such time," Halder wrote in his diary, "as hunger takes effect as our ally." Everyone else would take what Guderian, with feverish anticipation, had beckoned to all along as the "high road to Moscow." ✠

From a belfry high above captured Kiev, German soldiers gaze at the spires of the Pecherskaya Lavra, a Russian Orthodox monastery on the east bank of the Dnieper River. Upon entering Kiev, the Germans found and disarmed 10,000 mines left behind as booby traps in churches, museums, shops, and homes.

A Great City Marked for Death

Leningrad, the former czarist capital of St. Petersburg, was in many ways Russia's premier city. The "window on the West" opened by Peter the Great was a major seaport and a center of commerce and culture. But Hitler loathed the place as the crucible of the 1917 Bolshevik Revolution; his decision to blockade Leningrad and let its citizens starve to death subjected three million souls to one of the longest, most punishing sieges in human history. Nearly half the city's population died, most between the bitter months of October 1941 and April 1942. Those who endured became, in the words of one Leningrader, "animated corpses" living in a slow-motion world of hallucinatory unreality. "It seemed to us like a city at the bottom of the sea."

The siege began in mid-September, when the Germans cut rail lines into the city and occupied the surrounding territory. By November, virtually no food remained other than a gummy bread that bakers prepared from sawdust, moldy flour, and toxic cottonseed cake, originally intended as ship's fuel. The daily ration shrank to nine ounces of bread for manual laborers and half that much for everyone else. To supplement their diet, people scraped paste from wallpaper and bookbindings to make soup, used hair oil as cooking fat, and boiled leather belts and rat offal into jelly. Instances of cannibalism were reported.

Fuel soon became as scarce as food. Electricity was rationed and the city grew dark. As central heating systems shut down, plumbing pipes froze. Citizens drew their water from polluted ditches, canals, and the Neva River—shuffling back to their silent, frosty dwellings with the buckets slung from their necks because their hands lacked strength to clutch the handles.

By midwinter, 7,000 people were dying every day. Since there was no wood for coffins, the dead were shrouded in old curtains, rags, or wrapping paper; often they lay for weeks in their homes, on the street, or stacked in hospital corridors because the survivors were too frail to move them. The city fell into an eerie silence punctuated by the squeak of children's sleds— the only remaining means of transportation. Wrote a Russian journalist, "The city is dying as it has lived for the past half year—clenching its teeth."

A Russian antiaircraft gun trains beyond Leningrad's Saint Isaac

Cathedral toward the Germans outside the city. At its peak, the German force encircling Leningrad numbered 340,000 troops.

Daily Doses
of Bombs
and Shells

The wail of an air-raid siren, amplified over loudspeakers, sends citizens scurrying on a main street in Leningrad.

Nurses wearing steel helmets ▷ help passersby attend to a casualty of German shelling, a shopper whose precious bag of turnips lies spilled on the street.

Smoke and debris erupt from a Leningrad apartment building hit by a German bomb. During the first months of the siege, the Germans bombarded the city an average of nine hours each day.

ПЕРЕХОД

A Losing Struggle against the Cold

A worker tries to warm
his hands in an unheated
munitions plant whose
roof has been blown off.

Dragging firewood salvaged from ▷
a bombed building, a girl passes
a billboard proclaiming, "Death
to the murderers of children!"

The Grim Face of Famine

Women draw drinking water from a broken street main. Bodies disposed of in the city's river and canals gave the water an unforgettable taste.

A Leningrader clutches his daily ▷ bread. Starving young people sometimes robbed such older citizens of their rations.

Two women reap unexpected bounty by butchering a horse freshly killed by a German shell.

"Dying Is All That Happens Here"

Pedestrians stare mutely at a fellow citizen who has died on the snowy street. "In Leningrad," wrote a despondent diarist, "only one thing happens—dying."

A couple pulls a corpse on a ▷ sled down an icy street. "Taking someone to the cemetery," wrote a Leningrader, "exhausts the last vestiges of strength."

A convoy crawls over frozen Lake Ladoga, the only passage into Leningrad. Many trucks fell through the ice or were destroyed

by enemy fire, but enough crossed the "road of life" to sustain the city through the first terrible winter of the siege.

THREE

A Storm Aimed at Moscow

ieutenant Heinz-Otto Krause, a young company commander in the Ninth Army's sector of the eastern front, gave his men their orders at 5:40 on the morning of October 2, 1941. They would attack in five minutes—their objective a wooded area just ahead that was slowly becoming visible in the early light. The company would advance in ten files, with the ammunition carriers and heavy machine gunners in the middle of each. Krause reminded the troops that they were forbidden to attend the wounded or remove the dead until the engagement ended— and shirkers would be punished as usual, by being shot on the spot. "Now, good luck," he concluded, "and let us have a go at Ivan!" Ivan, it turned out, had the first go himself. Krause's company had advanced barely 300 yards when the Russians, hidden in the trees and under brush, opened fire with machine guns, rifles, and mortars. Krause shouted the order to charge and rushed forward with his men. Almost immediately, Germans and Russians were locked in vicious hand-to-hand combat. The woods echoed with the screams of the wounded and the dying. Suddenly, the Russians broke and ran, fleeing toward the shelter of the nearest town, Yartsevo, a cotton-milling center thirty miles northeast of Smolensk. The Germans pursued to the edge of Yartsevo, then set up their machine guns and peppered the town's wood-frame buildings, many of which were already burning following an air strike by Stukas.

With the day's first objective in hand, Lieutenant Krause ordered a halt and issued his panting troops an extra ration of schnapps. He took a swig himself as he rested beneath a birch tree with his first sergeant, a veteran named Bergmann. So far, so good.

"Well, Bergmann," said Krause, according to a postwar interview, "if our luck holds, Adolf will soon be standing atop the Kremlin's walls, with his right arm stretched out over Red Square."

"Yes, Lieutenant," Bergmann replied, "and old Feddy von Bock will be standing there alongside him. Word is that he is even more anxious to look down on Red Square than Adolf."

"Old Feddy" was, of course, Field Marshal Moritz Albrecht Franz

Panzer grenadiers lead a tank through the December gloom in 1941. "For only a few hours each day was there limited visibility at the front," a German officer recalled. "Until nine o'clock in the morning, the wintry landscape was shrouded in thick fog. At three o'clock in the afternoon, dusk set in, and an hour later it was dark again."

Friedrich Fedor von Bock, the aristocratic Prussian who commanded Army Group Center. Hitler's Directive 34 had been a bitter pill for the proud Bock. He had been stripped of his armor and instructed to content himself with local gains around Smolensk while the weight of Operation Barbarossa shifted to his flanks—to Army Group North, advancing on Leningrad, and Army Group South, driving into the Ukraine and the Crimea. Bock protested vigorously, directing his ire at his immediate superiors, Field Marshal Walther von Brauchitsch and General Franz Halder, whom he accused of robbing him of victory by not standing up to the Führer.

Now Bock was prepared to set differences aside. The army high command had given him the go-ahead to commit Krause's infantry company and hundreds like it to a new offensive. Operation Typhoon, an all-out attack on Moscow, proclaimed by Adolf Hitler to be the "last decisive battle of the year," had begun.

The Führer's forecast proved accurate enough—but not in the way he meant it. Operation Typhoon would be a deadly whirlwind for the Russians, but its harsh winds would also lash the Germans, whose suffering would be matched by few other armies in all of history. A time of unprecedented trial lay immediately ahead—and not only on the roads to Moscow. Drenching autumn rains would soon bring on the *Rasputitza*, the season of mud, and behind it loomed the fearsome Russian winter. On the northern front, German troops would batter themselves bloody trying to close the corridor connecting Leningrad and the main Russian line. In the south, there would be victories, then disappointment, as the quest for the Crimea fell short of complete success and the campaign for Rostov, gateway to the Caucasus, ended in retreat.

In preparation for Operation Typhoon, the army high command returned to Bock the forces taken from him in August, augmented by some new panzer units. By late September, Army Group Center totaled roughly 1.5 million men and more than 1,000 tanks. The troops were divided among Bock's three infantry armies, the Second, Fourth, and Ninth, and three panzer groups—the bulk of General Hermann Hoth's mobile units of Panzer Group 3, recalled from Army Group North; General Heinz Guderian's Panzer Group 2, strengthened by an extra armored corps from Army Group South; and General Erich Hoepner's Panzer Group 4, transferred from Army Group North. Thus reinforced, Bock controlled fourteen of the nineteen panzer divisions in Russia, eight of the fourteen motorized infantry divisions, and forty-eight divisions of regular infantry. In addition, he could count on the 1,000 airplanes of Field Marshal Albert Kesselring's Luftflotte 2, by far the largest Luftwaffe concentration on the eastern front.

A Classic Double Envelopment

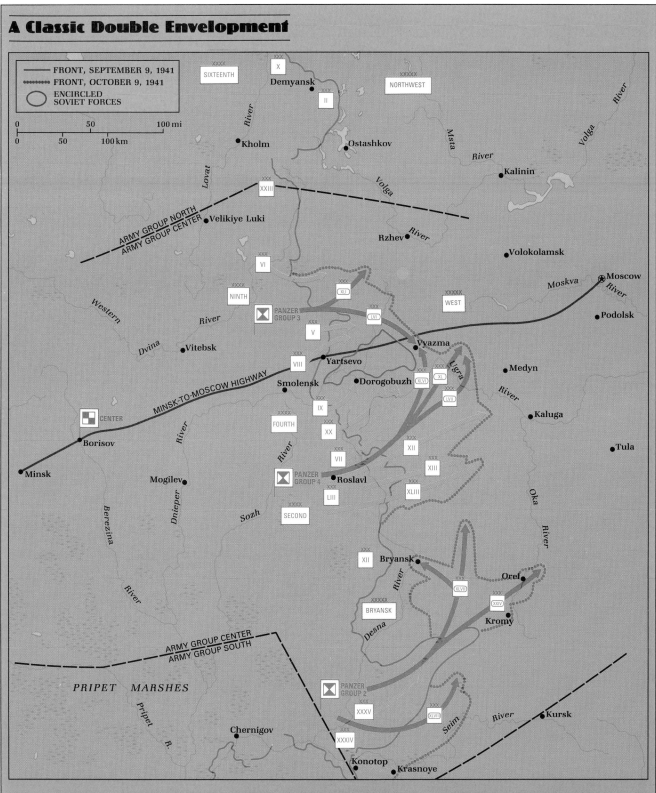

FRONT, SEPTEMBER 9, 1941
FRONT, OCTOBER 9, 1941
ENCIRCLED SOVIET FORCES

| 0 | 50 | 100 mi |

| 0 | 50 | 100 km |

ARMY GROUP NORTH
ARMY GROUP CENTER

SIXTEENTH

X

Demyansk

NORTHWEST

II

Kholm

Ostashkov

Kalinin

River

River

Msta

River

Volga

River

Lovat

XXIII

Velikiye Luki

ARMY GROUP NORTH
ARMY GROUP CENTER

Rzhev

Volokolamsk

River

Moskva

Moscow

River

VI

NINTH

PANZER GROUP 3

XLI

LVI

WEST

Podolsk

Western

River

Dvina

Vitebsk

VIII

Yartsevo

Vyazma

Ugra

Medyn

V

Smolensk

Dorogobuzh

XLVI

XL

LVII

River

Kaluga

CENTER

IX

XII

Tula

Borisov

FOURTH

XX

XIII

River

River

VII

XLIII

Oka

Minsk

Mogilev

Roslavl

River

PANZER GROUP 4

LIII

SECOND

Dnieper

Berezina

River

Sozh

XII

Bryansk

Orel

River

Desna

BRYANSK

XLVII

XXIV

Kromy

MINSK-TO-MOSCOW HIGHWAY

ARMY GROUP CENTER
ARMY GROUP SOUTH

PRIPET MARSHES

PANZER GROUP 2

XXXV

XLVIII

Seim

River

Kursk

Pripet

R.

Chernigov

XXXIV

Konotop

Krasnoye

The quiet west of Moscow ended on September 30, 1941, when General Fedor von Bock's Army Group Center, headquartered at Borisov, launched Operation Typhoon. The attack surprised the Russians. Bock's armor (*dark red*)—Guderian's Panzer Group 2 in the south, Hoepner's Panzer Group 4 in the center, and Hoth's Panzer Group 3 in the north—sliced around the flanks and between two Red Army groups. In a week, they had encircled six Soviet armies west of Vyazma and were forcing three others into pockets southwest and northeast of Bryansk. The double envelopment netted 673,000 prisoners. But eliminating the pockets tied down most of Bock's infantry until late October, and many Soviet soldiers slipped out of the noose, escaping eastward to help defend the Mozhaisk Line in front of Moscow. Others disappeared into the forests to form partisan bands that would harass Bock's increasingly precarious supply lines.

Civilian conscripts, most of them women, prepare earthen defenses west of Moscow. Working in shifts around the clock, 500,000 laborers dug 60 miles of antitank ditches and thousands of miles of trenches and strung 150 miles of barbed wire.

Bock's numbers, however, were deceiving. Three and a half months of campaigning had taken its toll, and none of the units were at full strength. By late September, overall German casualties stood at 534,000. Few divisions were even 80 percent whole, and most panzer regiments were at 75 percent strength or less. The men were weary, dirty, and often hungry.

Worse, Bock had never solved his problem of logistics. He was now 400 miles from his supply bases in Poland and required thirty trainloads of supplies each day to meet his huge consumption needs and to build up stocks for the offensive. Even after the Orsha-to-Smolensk railroad was converted to the narrower German gauge, supplies regularly fell 20 to 40 percent short of target. Fuel for tanks and other motorized vehicles was a particular problem. Motor oil, tires, and spare parts also were critically short. Fifteen days before Typhoon was to begin, Field Marshal Günther Hans von Kluge, commanding the Fourth Army, wrote: "The army is almost completely dependent on the railways. At the moment, the latter meet current consumption only. The army lives from hand to mouth." In order to stockpile as much fuel as possible, Bock cut back on food shipments, forcing the men either to live in part off the land or to tighten their belts.

On September 29, the day before their panzers and dive bombers were to launch Typhoon, Bock and Kesselring examined German aerial reconnaissance reports. They saw many changes. Throughout the August-September lull, the Russians had been busy shoring up the defenses in front of Moscow. Red Army labor battalions had constructed three long belts of antitank ditches, backed by field fortifications, across the anticipated German lines of advance, and artillerists had sunk heavy guns into bombproof earthen emplacements. The first line ran near Vyazma, an important rail center 135 miles southwest of Moscow. The inner defenses, called the Mozhaisk Line after the town at their center, had been dug largely by women and old men. Other changes were not visible from the air. The Russians had sown tens of thousands of land mines. And Stalin's generals, drawing on their strategic reserve, had massed nearly a quarter of a million soldiers at the defenses. They would soon be joined by fresh divisions from as far away as Siberia.

Later that day, Bock gathered his surly senior commanders. "The question arose," recalled General Günther Blumentritt, chief of staff of Kluge's Fourth Army, "whether sufficient time remained for us to capture Moscow with the weakened forces at our disposal before the Russian winter set in." Mindful of the weather and of his limited fuel supplies, Bock set November 7 as the deadline for investing the Soviet capital. After the meeting, he composed a message to the troops: "Soldiers of Army Group Center, after weeks of waiting, the army group renews the attack! Our objectives are

none other than the destruction of the remaining enemy forces to the east of us and the capture of the citadel of bolshevism—Moscow. I am confident that you will perform your duties as faithfully and bravely as you have done in the past. Let us not falter. Let us march to final victory!"

The attack began as a textbook blitzkrieg. After a warm sun broke through an autumnal haze, the weather turned ideal for tanks and planes, and during the first days of October, Bock's armor shoved back the Red Army, hitting with a speed and ferocity that recalled the successes of June. Kesselring's Stukas and twin-engine medium bombers flew thousands of sorties, disrupting Red Army troop concentrations and hammering enemy airstrips and strongpoints. On the ground, Guderian's panzers moved first, despite Guderian's protest that he needed more time to prepare. Only 50 of the 300 replacement tanks he had been promised arrived, and he had barely half of his promised fuel supplies. Cutting past the flank of the Russian Thirteenth Army south of Bryansk, his armored units advanced fifty miles on the first day. By October 3, they had reached the outskirts of Orel, an industrial center 130 miles in the Soviet rear. Streetcars were still running as the panzers rumbled into the town, and machinery from its factories lay stacked in great piles, waiting to be transported to the east.

The panzers farther north, attacking on October 2, also surprised the Russians, who could not believe Bock had realigned his forces so readily. By evening of the first day, tanks and infantry of Hoepner's Panzer Group 4 had elbowed aside the Soviet units guarding the Desna river crossing southeast of Smolensk and were soon rolling up the enemy defenses, twenty miles behind the front. Lieut. General Heinrich von Vietinghoff's XLVI Panzer Corps moved northeast toward Vyazma, and General Adolf Kuntzen's LVII Corps headed for Moscow. To Hoepner's north, beyond Smolensk, Hoth's Panzer Group 3 also broke through. Lieut. General Georg-Hans Reinhardt's XLI Panzer Corps slanted to the northeast, and the LVI Panzer Corps, led by Lieut. General Ferdinand Schaal, closed in on Vyazma.

Another devastating German encirclement was shaping up—or rather, two of them. While some of Guderian's panzers drove straight for Orel and beyond, his 17th Panzer Division and Lieut. General Joachim Lemelsen's XLVII Panzer Corps curled behind Bryansk. At the same time, the eight infantry divisions of General Maximilian Freiherr von Weichs's Second Army fought their way to the north of the city. On October 6, some of Weichs's infantry linked up with the vanguard of Guderian's panzers, trapping an entire Soviet army and parts of two others in two separate pockets north and south of Bryansk.

Meanwhile, the greater part of Hoepner's Panzer Group 4 linked up with

Launching Operation Typhoon, German infantrymen roll an antitank gun onto a dinghy to float it across the Desna River, while others (*background*) cross on a bridge of dinghies and planks. The retreating Russians had mined and damaged the railway trestle at rear.

Schaal's LVI Corps at Vyazma, thus cutting off the escape of the Russian armies that had massed to defend the Smolensk-to-Moscow highway. Even by Wehrmacht standards, the bag of prisoners was huge: at least forty-five divisions, 673,000 troops. In addition, the Germans seized or destroyed 1,200 tanks and 4,000 artillery pieces. By any measure, the victories at Bryansk and Vyazma constituted one of the most devastating double envelopments in military history.

Reducing the pockets, however, required precious time. The Soviet units trapped near Vyazma surrendered on October 17, but those in the larger pocket at Bryansk resisted furiously, and many thousands of men escaped to fight again. The last Red Army defenders at Bryansk did not give up until October 25. By then, the petrol pinch had begun to slow Bock's mechanized units. South of Orel, Lieut. General Werner Kempff's XLVIII Panzer Corps stopped to await fuel convoys, which now had to share the roads with hoards of Russian prisoners being marched in the opposite direction. To

make matters worse, on the night of October 6 the season's first snow fell, and, although it melted quickly, it was followed by rain. The precipitation combined with the massive weight of nonstop military traffic to churn the unpaved roads into glutinous mud.

Yet by mid-October, Bock's Army Group Center seemed poised for a climactic drive on Moscow. Although scattered Red Army units were still capable of resisting, the main Russian mobile reserve covering the direct approaches to the capital had been obliterated. German tanks, with their accompanying motorized infantry, had breached Moscow's westernmost defensive line. Hitler, however, created a fresh problem for his invasion force. Repeating his notion that Moscow itself was not important, the Führer demanded that the northern and southern arms of the offensive bypass the capital and continue around it to the east. Guderian's tanks were already headed roughly that way. Hitler's directive meant that elements of Panzer Group 3, now commanded by Lieut. General Georg-Hans Reinhardt—Hoth having been transferred to Army Group South—had to veer north from Vyazma toward Rzhev and the upper Volga River. Their objective was the large industrial city of Kalinin. This was a long detour— Kalinin was 100 miles northwest of Moscow.

Hitler's order robbed Bock's main thrust of one-third of its armor. By pooling his fuel reserves, Reinhardt managed to send a motorized infantry

After ramming a Russian T-34 tank, crew members of a German assault gun—two of them with head wounds from the collision—pry open the turret (*left*) and haul out a tanker (*below*)—one of 673,000 Russians captured in the Bryansk-Vyazma pockets.

battalion, reinforced by a panzer company, rumbling down the wide avenues of Kalinin on October 13. But his men were now no nearer the Soviet capital than they had been at Vyazma.

Nevertheless, Bock's armies were making progress, despite rain and mud and excessive detours. In Guderian's sector, a brigade-size battle group led by Colonel Hans Eberbach, consisting of all the armor of XXIV Corps that could be fueled, advanced toward Tula, a manufacturing center 105 miles south of Moscow. Panzer Group 3 pushed on and established a bridgehead on the east side of the Volga River. Meanwhile, Hoepner's Panzer Group 4

advanced on Mozhaisk and Yaroslavets. But, as these units aligned themselves for the final push, the weather worsened. Heavy rain and sleet, driven by bone-chilling winds, poured from the skies. The dirt roads became quagmires; streams and canals overflowed into the fields. The paving on the Smolensk-to-Moscow highway broke up under the relentless pounding of the tanks and other heavy vehicles.

Everywhere, German units slowed to a crawl. Trucks carrying troops and supplies sank axle deep and could be moved only by heavy tractors. "Even the supposedly first-class roads are practically impassable," Bock wrote in his war diary. "If a single supply truck gets through, the men consider it an achievement." In some places, artillery horses sank to their bellies in the slime. Where the footing was better, ten horses were needed to pull even a light gun through the mud. The German army wagons, their wheels and axles not built for such conditions, simply fell apart. Increasingly, the troops confiscated high-slung peasant carts called *Panjes* to carry their gear. Their well-bred German, Hungarian, and Belgian army horses died by the thousands from lack of fodder, and the Germans replaced them with hardy little native farm horses, which grazed on everything from birch twigs to the thatched roofs of peasant huts.

A German motorcyclist *(right)* and a squad of soldiers *(far right)* struggle to free their machines during the *Rasputitza*, the season of mud, brought on by autumn rains. "We had read about it in our studies of Russian conditions," wrote a vexed German officer, "but the reality far exceeded our worst expectations."

As the supply system threatened to collapse, the troops often went without rations. The men subsisted on potatoes and whatever other edibles they could scrounge. Here and there, tanks and other tracked vehicles moved ahead fitfully; German troops, with infinite labor, corduroyed mile after mile of road with tree trunks. But mostly, it was the infantry that trudged forward, the men soaked to the skin, their rotting calf-length boots often sucked off their feet by the gluelike muck.

Despite the abominable conditions, Army Group Center moved ahead. In the south, Brigade Eberbach closed in on Tula. Battling mud and the enemy, the Germans slogged to within three miles of the city. There, the Russians stopped them with 85-mm antiaircraft guns that knocked out more than twenty panzers.

The most promising advance came in the center. After defeating a Russian counterattack near Borovsk, Kuntzen's LVII Panzer Corps and infantry from Kluge's Fourth Army assaulted the second set of Soviet earthworks, the so-called Mozhaisk Line. Infantry from three motorized divisions fought through a maze of minefields and camouflaged pillboxes to surprise the defenders from the rear. Then tanks of the 19th Panzer Division, able to move because a temporary cold spell had frozen the ground, broke

through. By nightfall, the tanks had advanced forty miles, taking Borovsk and the bridge over the Protva River. Pressing on, some of the panzer units, carrying infantrymen on the tanks, reached the Nara River, sixty miles from Moscow. By October 18, Lieut. General Georg Stumme's XL Panzer Corps took Mozhaisk, on the Moskva River, and pushed on to the famed Napoleonic battlefield at Borodino.

In the south, the outlook for the invaders was less encouraging. Guderian's forces, beset by fuel shortages and a thaw, came to a standstill. When the weather to the north warmed up, the resulting mud halted Kuntzen's and Stumme's panzers in front of Moscow. By now, though, it was not just mud that slowed the German advance. In early October, Premier Stalin had entrusted the defense of Moscow to General Georgy Zhukov, who was emerging as one of Russia's best soldiers. Zhukov received well-trained army divisions from the country's vast interior to bolster the hastily formed units that had rushed to the capital's defense. He fed the fresh troops into his lines judiciously, using them to counter only the worst German threats. "With amazement and disappointment, we discovered that the beaten Russians seemed quite unaware that as a military force they had almost ceased to exist," Günther Blumentritt wrote. "During these weeks, enemy

The sea of mud made movement impossible for any kind of transport. Draft horses collapsed from exhaustion (left), tracked vehicles slued to a halt (center), and infantrymen had their boots sucked from their feet (right).

resistance stiffened, and with each day the fighting became bitterer."

In late October, German soldiers of the 98th Infantry Division, trying to hold the Nara River bridgehead near Borodino, tangled for the first time with troops from Siberia. Near Kalinin, General Adolf Strauss's Ninth Army met other troops from the east. German intelligence officers, questioning prisoners dressed in thick, quilted uniforms, were astonished to discover their captives were natives of Soviet Asia who spoke little or no Russian.

The Germans also encountered the formidable T-34 and KV-1 tanks, many of them fresh off the production line. The Russians loosed them against Guderian's spearhead at Venev and Stalinogorsk. The new tanks helped to stop the German advance, then pushed it back. Veteran panzer troops were horrified to see the big T-34s, riding on wide tracks but possessing a low center of gravity, sluing atop mud that trammeled their own tanks. And the German antitank detachments discovered that their 37-mm guns were useless against the T-34s. Only the Luftwaffe's powerful 88-mm flak guns, or courageous foot soldiers armed with mines and demolition charges, could stop the steel monsters.

After these desperate late-October battles at Stalinogorsk, Tula, Borodino, and Kalinin, the German offensive dwindled across its entire

General Georgy Zhukov *(right)*, appointed by Josef Stalin to command Russia's crumbling western front, studies a message tape with his chief of staff, Lieut. General Vasily Sokolovsky *(left)*, and Deputy Premier Nikolay Bulganin *(center)*.

400-mile front. Almost within sight of Moscow in places, Bock's troops were hopelessly bogged down. Artillerymen had few shells; panzer crews had to siphon the tiny quantities of fuel left in several tanks in order to gas up one; and the infantrymen were completely spent, short of ammunition and food. As Bock's men drew from their last reserves of energy and will power, a lull settled over the front.

Bock now hoped for a freeze that would harden the ground and let the tanks move ahead once more. But several of his subordinate commanders, notably Hoepner, favored postponing further attacks and digging in for the winter. After all, Barbarossa had accomplished much. The German armies had sustained one of the greatest offensives ever and killed or captured as many Russians as there were Germans in the invading armies. But Bock and, more important, Hitler would hear none of that. Bock remained determined to reach Moscow and finish the long campaign for which so much had been sacrificed. Clearly, to go on was a terrible gamble. Would the German men and machines be able to operate in the frightful Russian cold? No one knew, but the alternatives—to retreat and risk being caught in exposed positions, or to ride out the winter—seemed even less attractive.

During August and September, while Bock steamed with frustration at Smolensk, Field Marshal Gerd von Rundstedt, commander of Army Group South, had advanced across the Ukraine toward objectives that Hitler considered more important than Moscow. They included Kharkov, the Soviet Union's fourth largest city; the coal and iron industries of the Donets Basin; the Crimea; and, finally, the oil fields of the Caucasus. On the far northern end of the front, Rundstedt's main tank force, Panzer Group 1 under General Ewald von Kleist, had crossed the Dnieper River early in September and turned north to reach the open country east of Kiev. At the same time, Guderian's tanks raced southward, covering 250 miles in only two weeks. By mid-September, the two panzer forces, supported by three field armies, had closed a huge 130-mile-deep ring around 800,000 Russian troops and vast numbers of Soviet tanks and guns. During the great encirclement battle of Kiev, Rundstedt had torn a huge hole in the Russian defenses. Through it he poured the Sixth Army, led by Field Marshal Walther von Reichenau, and the Seventeenth Army, under Lieut. General Karl-Heinrich von Stülpnagel. The two infantry armies advanced into the eastern Ukraine, heading for Kharkov and the Donets Basin. Also free to move was Kleist's Panzer Group 1, which turned southeast, toward the Sea of Azov and the city of Rostov *(map, page 120)*.

In the south, Rundstedt also made swift progress. Engineers and assault

Russian factory workers ride a T-34 tank off an assembly line in the Ural Mountains. The T-34 became a problem for the Germans, who had underestimated the Soviets' ability to mass-produce high-quality tanks.

troops of the Eleventh Army's 22d Lower Saxon Division threw a pontoon bridge almost half a mile long across the lower Dnieper in the face of savage Russian fire—an astonishing feat of military engineering. Across the bridge tramped the LIV Infantry Corps and the Rumanian Third Army. These units then fanned out to cover the approaches to Rostov and the Crimea. On October 6, Kleist's command, now upgraded to First Panzer Army, linked up with the Eleventh Army near the village of Osipenko, on the shore of the Sea of Azov. Kleist then turned east, toward Rostov and the Caucasus. During this encircling maneuver, the Germans netted 106,000 prisoners.

All was going according to plan, but stubborn Russian resistance—and the weather—soon made trouble. The first setback came during the second week in September, when the Eleventh Army tried to take the Perekop Isthmus by a swift coup. In the lead were motorcyclists and armored cars of the Leibstandarte Adolf Hitler, the Waffen-SS brigade that a few months earlier had distinguished itself in action against the Greeks during the Balkan campaign. Approaching a village on the main road to the Perekop Isthmus—the only suitable route onto the Crimean Peninsula—the SS reconnaissance unit received a bizarre warning that the Russians were ready. When the forward motorcyclists drove a flock of sheep off the road into the bordering fields, the unfortunate beasts set off dozens of land mines. Almost at once, the unit came under raking fire from a Russian armored train standing on tracks beyond the village and from riflemen and machine gunners concealed in foxholes. Several Germans were killed. The others hit the dirt and then, covered by the 20-mm cannons of their armored cars, scrambled to the rear. The Germans threw up a smoke screen, enabling a few brave cyclists to dash forward and recover the wounded. Assessing the situation, the officer in charge, Major Kurt Meyer, notified his superiors, "Coup against Perekop impossible."

General Erich von Manstein—newly in command of the Eleventh Army after his predecessor, General Eugen Ritter von Schobert, was killed landing his scout plane in another Russian minefield—concentrated a large force for a second attack on the isthmus. To lead the assault, he chose the two infantry divisions of Lieut. General Erik Hansen's LIV Corps, with another division, the 50th, added for extra punch. All available Eleventh Army engineers, artillery, and flak units were ordered to support the infantry. In ready reserve would be General Josef Kübler's XLIX Mountain Corps and the Leibstandarte Adolf Hitler.

Manstein realized that he could not capture all of the Crimea with the limited number of troops at his disposal, but he hoped to prevent the defenders of the Perekop line from reinforcing the Black Sea port of Sevastopol, which boasted a huge citadel. If the German units moved fast

Their helmets glinting in the Arctic sun, gunners in a Munich flak regiment—part of the northernmost element of the German invasion force (map, inset)—fire their 88-mm gun from the Rybachi Peninsula, a projection into the Barents Sea northwest of Murmansk.

Frustration in the Arctic

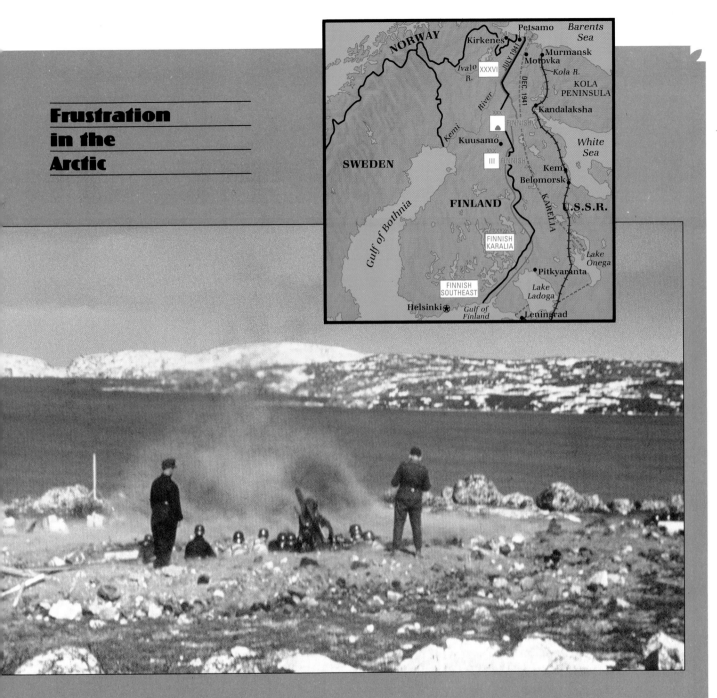

In the summer of 1941, a sixty-mile stretch of Arctic wasteland frustrated German aggression more effectively than Belgian forests, Greek mountains, and North African desert ever had. Six German and Finnish divisions set out from Finland to capture the ice-free port of Murmansk, the Soviet Union's backdoor to the Atlantic, north of the Arctic Circle on the Barents Sea, and to sever the railroad linking it to Leningrad, 625 miles to the south. But the desolate, roadless tundra that separated the attackers from their objectives prevented them from replenishing supplies or bringing up reserves and artillery.

The Germans and Finns were forced to deliver every shell and loaf of bread in horse-drawn wagons, then by pack mule, and finally on the backs of the soldiers themselves. Instead of fighting, entire battalions were diverted to hand-carry the wounded on arduous ten-hour treks to the rear. By contrast, the Russians fought with the railway and a passable road at their backs and transported vital supplies and fresh soldiers directly to the battlefield.

After three assaults, the Germans were still twenty-eight miles from Murmansk, and when the first snows blanketed the treeless plain in late September, Hitler's northernmost troops grudgingly went on the defensive. Their failure affected all of Operation Barbarossa: Over the next three years, a stream of ships bearing Allied aid nosed into the docks at Murmansk, making good Soviet losses and fortifying the Russians for ultimate victory.

The Drive to the Don

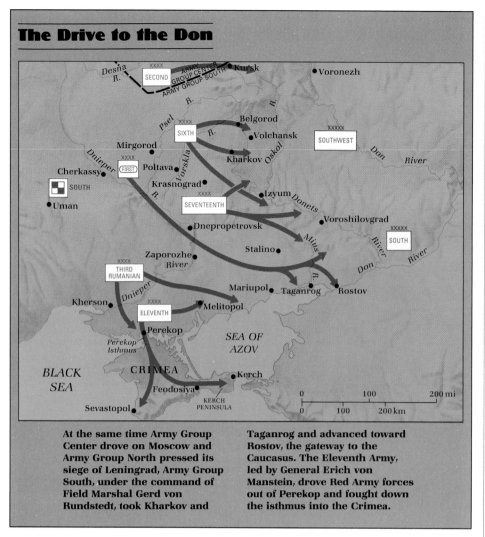

Mules and men of the XLIX Mountain Corps cross the Dnieper River in the eastern Ukraine on a 500-yard-long pontoon bridge built by German engineers on September 1, 1941. The half-submerged ambulance at center had been blown off the bridge during a Soviet air strike.

enough, they might be able to seize this fortress before the disorganized defenders could react. Just as Manstein began the attack, he found his left flank and rear threatened by two Russian armies. Striking at the parts of the front held by the Rumanian Mountain Corps, the Soviets tore a gap ten miles wide in one spot and made dangerous penetrations in two others. Suddenly, Manstein's entire army was in danger of being cut off. He quickly turned around Kübler's mountain corps and the Leibstandarte and called for help. Fortunately, the III Panzer Corps, under Lieut. General Eberhard von Mackensen, had nearly reached its staging area for the advance on Rostov. Mackensen's tanks fell upon the exposed flank and rear of the Russian armies, dispatching them in headlong retreat.

At the same time, troops of the Leibstandarte rushed through a gap in the lines of the Russian Ninth Army, capturing most of its headquarters staff. SS reconnaissance troops then sped toward the city of Mariupol. A German motorcyclist named Wontorra recalled driving to the crest of a hill and seeing the city below. Racing down the slope, Wontorra and his cyclists wove past antitank obstacles, stopping only when they reached the first main intersection. From there, joined by Leibstandarte armored cars, they sped on, machine-gunning and dispersing a Cossack cavalry detachment bivouacked in a park. "In one spot, the road sloped down sharply and was filled to overflowing with Russian soldiers. We halted briefly while our *Sturmgeschütz* (assault gun) pulled up just behind us and fired a shell down the street." Soon, Wontorra recalled, "the Russian soldiers disappeared, and Mariupol, a city of almost 250,000 people, was in our hands."

The Perekop Isthmus was so narrow—less than five miles wide—that the Germans had no room for maneuver. And the cramped corridor was intricately fortified and packed with defenders. In order to break through to the Crimea, Manstein had no choice but to mount a frontal assault. His main attack began at five in the morning on October 18 with a powerful artillery barrage. Shells exploded only 100 yards in front of the waiting assault troops. Then, in World War I fashion, the barrage lifted briefly before beginning again, the shells this time falling farther back in the Russian

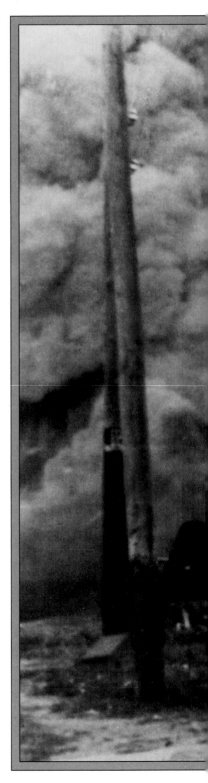

defenses. This was the signal for the infantry to leap forward. Men in the first line dodged ahead in short rushes while the machine gunners and mortar crews tried to keep the Russian defenders down.

The Soviets fought back with withering fire. Machine guns rattled from reinforced dugouts untouched by the bombardment, and artillery pounded planned zones of fire. The Germans soon found themselves in deadly tangles of barbed wire, mines, concrete pillboxes, hidden flame throwers, and even buried sea mines that the Russians detonated by remote control.

Advancing on the flank of the stalled 47th Infantry Division, the 22d Infantry Division seized a fortified ridge—one of the few areas of elevated terrain. But enemy fire soon forced the Germans to dig in. Pinned down, the 47th Division suffered heavy casualties. As night fell, the men spaded watery foxholes in the marshy ground. The battle continued the next day and the day after in rain and fog that concealed the Russian positions.

Yard by yard, the Germans moved forward. Manstein had no tanks, so he used self-propelled guns to crush obstacles and shell pillboxes. He ordered a final all-out punch for October 28. That day, the self-propelled guns and the 170th Infantry on the far right broke through, and retreating Soviet troops streamed southward toward Sevastopol. Still, conquest of the Crimea was far from assured. To follow Hansen's depleted LIV Corps, Manstein had only one other corps of foot soldiers, the XXX. His lone motorized unit, the Leibstandarte, and the well-equipped XLIX Mountain Corps had been sent with Kleist toward Rostov. Manstein's chief of staff, Colonel Otto Wöhler, proposed an ingenious tactic. Wöhler strung together a fast-moving combat group consisting of the only serviceable vehicles the two infantry corps still possessed, along with those from the reconnaissance detachments and the motorized antiaircraft and antitank units. As this force sped ahead, the Germans cut off most of the remaining Russians. By November 16, they had rounded up more than 100,000 prisoners.

A sizable number of Soviet troops had made it to the citadel at Sevastopol, where they could be supplied by sea. Manstein tried one attack on the outer works of the fortress and concluded that it could be taken only after a carefully prepared siege. It would be five months before the next German attacks began, and many more before the citadel fell.

Hard fighting to the east paralleled Manstein's slugging match on the Perekop Isthmus. In a five-day battle in mid-October near the Sea of Azov, the 3d Company of the Leibstandarte Adolf Hitler's infantry regiment lost all but seven of its 100-plus men. Nevertheless, the Leibstandarte and Kleist's panzer and motorized divisions took the port of Taganrog and crossed the Mius River, the last major barrier on the way to Rostov.

Farther north, other parts of Army Group South, though delayed by rain and mud, also made headway. Field Marshal Walther von Reichenau's Sixth Army took Kharkov on October 24 and crossed the Donets River. On Reichenau's right flank, Stülpnagel's Seventeenth Army moved into the Donets Basin—and found much of the industrial machinery gone. The Russians had shipped entire factories to new sites in the Ural Mountains.

Cheated of the anticipated spoils of the Donets, Hitler was all the more determined that Rundstedt's weary armies fulfill the next part of his master plan—the conquest of the Caucasus. But the weather intervened, just as it had on the road to Moscow. The rains created lakes of mud, swallowing troops and equipment. Kleist's panzers had to use so many peasant carts to haul supplies, remarked the army's quartermaster general, that they should be called *Panje*, not panzer, divisions.

In mid-November, bitter cold arrived, freezing the ground. Kleist immediately dispatched the III Panzer Corps toward Rostov. The Leibstandarte, reinforced by the 13th Panzer Regiment, took the lead, followed by the 13th and 14th Panzer Divisions and the 60th Motorized Infantry Division. Savage fighting marked the way. The SS troops clawed into the city's outskirts house by house. Counterattacking T-34 tanks rolled over the German motorized infantry's antitank guns, reducing them to tangled scrap. Eventually, however, the panzers broke through, and on November 20 they stormed into the city. The Leibstandarte captured a vital railroad bridge spanning the Don River; the motorized infantry and one panzer division pursued the retreating Russians to the southeast. The Germans now held not only the gateway to the Caucasus, but also southern Russia's key crossroads for supplies and oil moving north from Baku.

Almost at once, a Soviet army lying in wait beyond the Don counterattacked. Its infantry charged across the frozen river in long lines, and they kept coming despite deadly fire from German machine guns. Some Russians made it across, climbed the riverbank, and threw grenades among the German defenders before being driven off.

These suicidal charges were essentially a diversion, however. The real danger came from farther north, where three entire Russian armies—thirty-one divisions, along with five tank brigades—had been cobbled together during the previous month, partly through the organizational efforts of a military commissar by the name of Nikita Khrushchev. Starting southward on November 17, three days before Rostov fell, the leading Russian divisions skirted east of Reichenau's Sixth Army and around the Seventeenth Army as well, which could not struggle through the mud fast enough to cut the Soviets off.

The first attacks fell on the 60th Motorized Infantry Division northeast

Sixth Army troops pass steel tank traps as they enter the Ukrainian city of Kharkov in late October 1941. The metropolis was one of Hitler's primary targets, but the Germans captured little of value there because the Soviets had dismantled and evacuated most of the city's factories.

of Rostov. Kleist and Rundstedt realized immediately that their salient at Rostov was in danger of being pinched off. The Germans did not have enough men and tanks and ammunition to hold a front sixty miles long, and on November 28, Rundstedt ordered a withdrawal. The army high command gave its approval on November 30, but Hitler countermanded the OKH. Furious, Rundstedt demanded that he be removed from command. Hitler complied, replacing him with Reichenau. There would be no retreat, the Führer raged; Rostov must be held at all costs.

Reichenau, however, also saw the hopelessness of the situation and telephoned Hitler to beg permission to fall back. On December 1, Hitler relented, and the forces in and around Rostov moved to more defensible positions six miles in front of the Mius River. Despite the confusion caused by conflicting orders, most of the troops managed an orderly withdrawal. It was the first time the Red Army had mounted a counterattack that was at once large and well executed.

A more devastating withdrawal far to the north followed the Rostov retreat. The Leningrad front had remained largely static since Hoepner's Panzer Group 4 shifted south to reinforce Bock's drive on Moscow. The bulk of the Eighteenth Army continued to besiege the city while the Sixteenth Army held a line south from Lake Ilmen to the area around Ostashkov, where it touched the left flank of Army Group Center.

Nonetheless, an objective important to Hitler remained—the city of Tikhvin, a mining center for bauxite, a mineral used to manufacture aluminum, and a vital rail junction 115 miles east of Leningrad. The Russians sent supplies by rail through Tikhvin to the eastern shore of Lake Ladoga, and from there by barge to Leningrad. Now Lake Ladoga was freezing over. Before long, the Russians would be able to run convoys of trucks across the ice. The siege line around Leningrad would have a large hole in it unless Tikhvin and other transshipment points east of the lake and as far north as the Svir River were taken. In addition, the Germans hoped that their Finnish allies would advance around the lake from the north and link up with them at the Svir, tightening the ring.

Assigned the job of capturing Tikhvin was the XXXIX Panzer Corps, which comprised two panzer divisions and two divisions of motorized infantry, all under the command of General Rudolf Schmidt. Moving out on October 15, Schmidt's force passed through the Sixteenth Army's lines on the Volkhov River and headed into the taiga, an uncharted, subarctic wilderness consisting of marsh and coniferous forest. Schmidt sent out scouting parties to find paths for the tanks and trucks, and his corps lumbered forward. After more than three weeks, units of the 12th Panzer Division smashed into Tikhvin. The infantry took the western approaches while the panzers occupied the east side of town.

So far, everything had gone well, but the Russians were in no mood to allow Leningrad's sole lifeline to be choked off. On November 15, a fresh Siberian infantry division attacked the German perimeter. The Soviets were supported by a brigade partly equipped with T-34 tanks and by Katyusha rocket launchers that hurled thousands of pounds of explosives into the German positions. The 18th Artillery Regiment, which was attached to the German motorized infantry, knocked out fifty of the large Soviet tanks, but the Siberian riflemen kept coming.

The two German divisions held, but Tikhvin had been blasted into a smoldering ruin. More Siberian troops also attacked the XXXIX Panzer

Field Marshal Gerd von Rundstedt, commander of Army Group South, receives Hitler *(back to camera)* **at his Ukrainian headquarters in August 1941. Four months later, Hitler fired Rundstedt for advocating a retreat from Rostov.**

Corps's other two divisions, which had gone on to attempt a linkup with the Finns on the Svir River. It was soon clear to the new commander of the XXXIX Corps, Lieut. General Jürgen von Arnim, who had assumed command when Schmidt was sent south to replace the ailing General Weichs, that his corps was in a desperate situation, exposed without shelter to the brutal arctic winter and at the mercy of Soviet counterattacks. Ordering a retreat to the Volkhov, he started his men back across sixty-five miles of frozen swamps and wasteland.

Temperatures dropped to fifty-two degrees below zero. The German rear guard, the 11th and 12th Companies of the 51st Motorized Infantry, was all but wiped out fighting to buy time for their comrades' escape. The 18th Motorized Infantry Division had set out for Tikhvin in November 9,000 strong. When the division recrossed the Volkhov River on December 22, only 741 of its men remained.

By early November, the rutted ground on the approach to Moscow had frozen as hard as the forested swamps around Tikhvin. On November 15, Field Marshal Fedor von Bock sent Army Group Center lurching eastward again toward the capital city. The two-week hiatus had done his forces

German soldiers huddle over a fire in a trench dug before cold weather froze the ground. "In our hole," one veteran recalled, "we stood around the fire in our fur hats and earmuffs, gloves, two or three blankets, and a fur wrap, and it was still so cold you couldn't stand it."

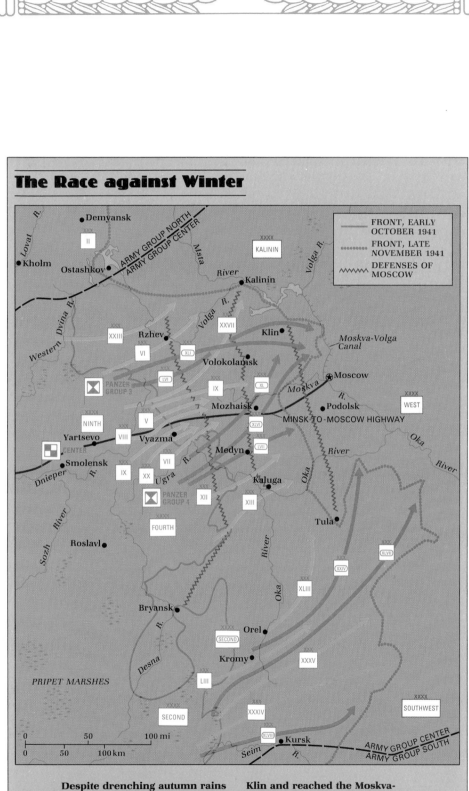

The Race against Winter

Despite drenching autumn rains that made the roads almost impassable, Bock's Army Group Center pushed doggedly toward Moscow. To the north, Reinhardt's Panzer Group 3 captured Kalinin, on the Volga River. Turning to the southeast, Reinhardt's panzers then took Klin and reached the Moskva-Volga Canal. Hoepner's Panzer Group 4 advanced along the Mozhaisk-to-Moscow highway. And to the south, Guderian's Second Panzer Army bypassed Tula, 120 miles from Moscow, as it tried to swing around the capital from the southwest.

some good—but not enough. His companies, battalions, and divisions, strung out and disorganized in the October mud, had been largely reassembled. Tanks, trucks, and guns had been hacked free from the frozen mud. Many were ruined in the process, but at least some of the units recouped part of their equipment.

Army Group Center would now pay the full price for its inadequate supply system. Although warm winter overcoats had been collected and shipped to Russian railheads, few of them reached the front. The men shivered miserably in their summer uniforms, now filthy and threadbare, as temperatures plummeted to zero and below. As the cold worsened, tank and truck engines would not start; sometimes they froze while running. Units that were able to obtain antifreeze discovered, to their dismay, that it, too, sometimes froze solid. Weapons became useless. Artillery, machine guns, and even rifles refused to fire for lack of low-temperature lubricants.

Few armies have been in poorer shape to undertake an offensive. Yet, as the November attacks began, the Germans forced the Russians back. In the forefront were Reinhardt's Panzer Group 3 and parts of Strauss's Ninth Army. Heading for Moscow's northwestern suburbs, they fought southeast from the Kalinin area. Within a week, Reinhardt's advance units had taken the ancient city of Klin and were pressing toward the Moskva-Volga Canal near Takhroma, only thirty-eight miles from the capital.

On November 16, Hoepner's Panzer Group 4, possessing barely 200 miles' worth of fuel, attacked in the center. Finding a weakly defended area, the 78th Storm Division of the IX Corps broke into the Russian rear, took prisoners, then kept rolling. Ten days later, Hoepner's tanks had advanced twenty-five miles and were thirty miles from Moscow. In the south, Guderian also attacked, trying once again to push past Tula and Stalinogorsk and move behind the Soviet capital.

The weather, however, was taking its inexorable toll. Nighttime temperatures sank to fifty degrees below zero, far colder than anyone in the German army could have imagined. A few fortunate troops found shelter in peasant huts. Frostbite became endemic, and the wounded died where they fell from shock exacerbated by the cold. In some places, the snow already was two feet deep.

These conditions—and furious counterattacks by fresh Russian troops—convinced Guderian that his forces could no longer continue to attack. But to the north, both Reinhardt and Hoepner were still advancing. Having taken Klin, Reinhardt's panzers moved on to Rogachevo, slicing between two Soviet armies and reaching the Moskva-Volga Canal. There, Colonel Hasso von Manteuffel, commanding a spearhead comprising the 6th Rifle Regiment and the 25th Panzer Regiment, seized a crossing and

established a bridgehead on the east bank. A detachment captured the power station that served Moscow. A direct route to the city lay open, but reinforcements could not get through to exploit the breakthrough. By the afternoon of November 27, the cold had become so paralyzing that the automatic weapons of Manteuffel's men would no longer fire.

Then, disaster. Out of a blinding fog of ice crystals emerged two brigades of the Soviet First Shock Army, infantrymen with an enlarged complement of artillery. The Russians wore heavy winter greatcoats, fur hats, and thick felt boots. They had mufflike coverings over their assault weapons, which were lubricated with cold-weather oil. Working through the snow, the Russians blasted one German outpost after another, backing up their infantry with T-34s. The Germans clung tenaciously to their bridgehead until November 29, when Manteuffel ordered a withdrawal, leaving a thin defensive line on the canal's west bank. The chance for a breakthrough to Moscow from the north had vanished.

All along the line, the German attacks slowed. A few miles south of the Moskva-Volga Canal, elements of Lieut. General Rudolf Veiel's 2d Panzer Division rumbled through a blizzard as far as Ozeretskoye, on the main road from Rogachevo to Moscow. There the troops found kiosks for commuter buses to the capital city and joked about riding the remaining twenty-four miles to Red Square.

Parts of Hoepner's Panzer Group 4 battled even closer. On November 29, several tank units broke into the western suburbs and reached Tushino, a section of Moscow proper. Others captured Krasnaya Polyana—the former country home of the great novelist Leo Tolstoy—and one battalion rolled as far as Gorki Leninskoye, twelve miles from the city limits. But Soviet reserves arrived; Siberian battalions were even driven to Gorki in taxis, much like French reinforcements for the Battle of the Marne in 1914.

A few miles farther north, two other corps from Panzer Group 4 also battled forward. Fighting in the lead, the 5th and 10th Panzer Divisions and the motorized SS division Reich plowed through forests and snowy fields, from one village to another, until they reached the Istra River where it widened into a reservoir. Under heavy fire, a motorcycle battalion crossed the ice and secured a foothold on the far bank for the larger units that followed. A combat group from the 10th Panzer Division assaulted Istra itself. Advancing still farther, a motorcycle detachment of the 38th Pioneer Battalion raced ahead to capture the railroad station at Lobnya and scout the area south of it. Finding no opposition, the pioneers blew up the station and roared forward to Khimki, a landing on the Moskva River five miles from the city line. This was as close as the Germans came before Soviet counterattacks rocked them back.

A German supply column plods doggedly along a wind-swept trail marked only by telephone poles. "The psychological effect of the country on the ordinary soldier was considerable," wrote a German general. "He felt small and lost in the endless space."

The advance along the Smolensk-to-Moscow highway also halted. The 3d Battalion, 478th Infantry Regiment, part of Kluge's Fourth Army, was more fortunate than most. The battalion had taken the village of Burzevo and holed up there. Dozens of men crowded into cramped peasant huts, warming themselves around the huge stoves. They piled bricks near the flames, and when time came to relieve the sentries, the men took hot bricks with them wrapped in rags, to thaw out their weapons.

For the troops left in the open, there was no escaping the frigid cold. Unable to hack any shelter in the rock-hard ground, they could only huddle together miserably in a vain attempt to maintain body heat. Thousands of them succumbed to frostbite. Many gave way to the strange euphoria that hypothermia produces just before unconsciousness. They simply crumpled in the snow and died.

On December 5, Kluge pulled the advance units of the Fourth Army behind the Nara River and unilaterally suspended offensive operations. The next day, Bock gave in and issued a similar order for the rest of Army Group Center. His force was too worn down to continue. A young second lieutenant in the 128th Army Artillery Regiment expressed the common frustration in a letter to his mother in Hamburg: "These Russians seem to have an inexhaustible supply of men. Here they unload fresh troops from Siberia every day; they bring up fresh guns and lay mines all over the place. On December 30, we made our last attack—a hill known to us as Pear Hill and a village called Lenino. With artillery and mortar support, we managed to take all of the hill and half of the village. But at night, we had to give it all up again in order to defend ourselves more effectively against the continuous counterattacks. We needed only another eight miles to get the capital within gun range—but we just could not make it." ✚

A German Soldier's Story

"Whenever German soldiers misbehaved," Wolfgang Horn remembered after the war, "the threat to send them to the Russian front cooled them off instantly." The Soviet Union's winters, its soldiers' reputation as implacable foes, and the land's size struck dread into German hearts.

The fears were well founded. Three hundred thousand soldiers who marched into Russia under the swastika in June 1941 were dead by the following spring. Horn, a twenty-two-year-old artilleryman in the 10th Panzer Division, survived. And unlike most veterans, who relied on memory and imagination, Horn had a record of the invasion. A diarist, letter writer, and photographer whose collapsible Voigtlaender Bessa camera was easy to stow, he chronicled the campaign in a journal and in photographs he sent home to Saxony. Horn's words and pictures are published here for the first time.

Initially part of Guderian's Panzer Group 2 and later in Hoepner's Panzer Group 4, Horn's division took part in Army Group Center's thrust to Moscow and the retreat that followed. Serving first as a surveyor for his battery, then as chief of a six-man gun crew, Horn was nearly killed early on and was wounded again during the October encirclement of Vyazma. There he earned an Iron Cross on what he described as the "most exciting day of my life."

Not all days were exciting. "War does not consist of continuous fighting, as many people assume," he wrote. His most vivid recollections are of scrounging for potatoes, mending his uniform, and scratching shelter in the frozen earth. Horn's odyssey ended in April 1942, when the remnants of his division were shifted to France. He and his comrades now wore a medal (page 166) created for survivors of the winter. They dubbed it the *Gefrierfleisch Orden*, or the Order of Frozen Flesh.

Sergeant Wolfgang Horn (*above, in 1942*) filled nine albums with photos of the Russian and other campaigns. The volume above bears the legend *War Memories*.

June 20, 1941. In a Polish forest across the Bug River from Brest-Litovsk, Horn (*foreground, photographed by a fellow soldier*) and another surveyor prepare maps for the June 22 bombardment of the Russian positions. "As the planned time approaches, we look at our watches. We know that thousands of guns will open fire at the same time along a thousand-mile front," he wrote.

June 28, 1941. A Ju 52 carrying supplies to a forward base flies over motorized infantry of the 10th Panzer speeding east on a road the Germans called *Rollbahn I*—one of Russia's few paved highways. Horn noted, "Along the road, we saw abandoned Russian equipment, from tanks to guns, and dead horses."

June 28, 1941. Russians watch German soldiers pull a field kitchen into Kopyl. "The villages all seemed poor. Flowers in tins in some windows looked pathetic. Gardens were scarce. But the clothing was a bit better than in Poland and the population mostly friendly, quite different from the glum Poles."

June 29, 1941. Captured Russian soldiers listen as one of their group is interrogated by German officers and an interpreter *(in trench coat)*. Reflecting on the courteous nature of this exchange—in stark contrast to the brutality both sides displayed later—Horn commented, "They were not yet used to this war, and neither were we."

June 30, 1941. German artillery vehicles, each marked with the letter *G,* designating them part of Guderian's panzer group, advance along a forest road. "Our division is now the spearhead," reported Horn. "Around three in the afternoon, we drive through woods still full of Russian troops, so we are ready to jump off with our rifles at the first shot and take cover."

June 30, 1941. In response to Russian shelling, a German gun crew hastily unlimbers its howitzer and returns fire.

July 1, 1941. "We pass through the agricultural-research estate of Zazierje," Horn recorded dutifully, "and drive over a wooden bridge across the Svisloch River, where Russian prisoners pass us on their way to the rear."

July 2, 1941 (dawn). Outside the city of Minsk, a howitzer crew duels with distant Russian guns. Not long after Horn took this picture, a shell struck one of the German cannons, blowing it up and wounding him.

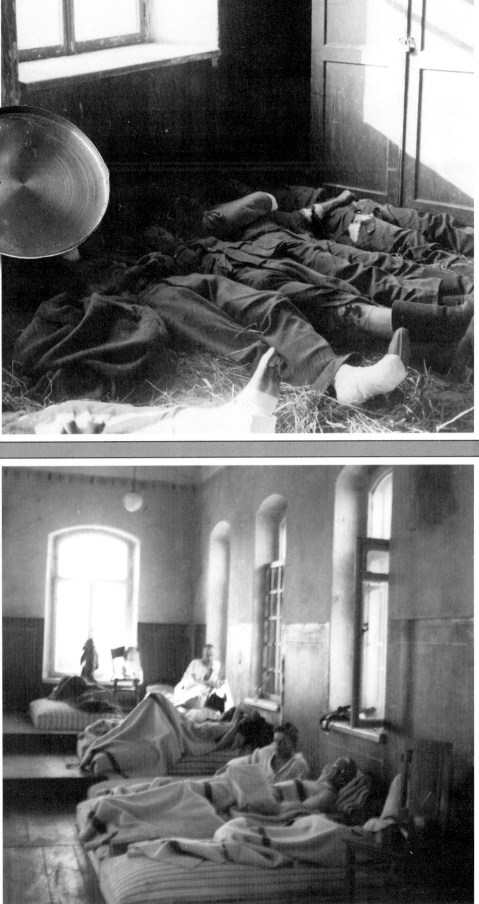

July 2, 1941 (midmorning). "The shell seems headed right at me," Horn wrote. "I feel doomed and duck forward. A crash. A fountain of earth rises in front of me. Something passes through my right forearm and upper leg, and I see blood seeping out. A shell fragment sticks out of my leg. I pull it out and it burns my fingers. I look at my field glasses. One side is practically destroyed. My leather map case is totally wrecked, and also my compass *(above)*, but these ruined items have protected my breast and groin."

July 2, 1941 (afternoon). "An ambulance brings us to Cherven. We are unloaded at an office and placed on straw spread on the floor *(above, right)*. More and more wounded are brought in—that day, about 280. No wonder the medics have little time for us! Since I have no blanket, I suffer from the cold at night. The next day, we get one blanket for two men."

July 4, 1941. "We are transferred to a field hospital *(right)*. I am put into a room with soiled mattresses on the floor and no linen. An insecticide is sprayed to ward off the hordes of flies. Russian orderlies distribute water, corn coffee, and food. My wounds are smeared with a cod-liver salve." Horn was sent home, but in August he rejoined his unit on the drive to Moscow.

August 31, 1941. For the price of a little bread, famished Polish youngsters (*above*) shine the boots of German soldiers in Brest-Litovsk, where the train returning Horn to Russia crossed the Bug River. Three days later, he arrived in Smolensk and began a four-day march to the front. "Singing our favorite songs —some quite sentimental, fitting the rainy days and monotonous landscape—playing games, and talking of food and sex helped us through the long journey."

October 8, 1941. Two German infantrymen (*left*), eyeing abandoned houses for snipers, pass a statue of Lenin in the main square of Vyazma. "I limp through some houses," wrote Horn. "Most civilians seem to have been evacuated. I find a clean shirt I can use, but nothing else useful, and nothing to eat."

October 16, 1941. With members of his battery, Horn (*far left*) huddles over a fire near Borodino, "a village known to us because of the narrow victory there of Napoléon's forces over Russians led by General Kutuzov in 1812. The victory allowed Napoléon to occupy Moscow—just seventy miles away."

October 22, 1941. Returning from a sortie, a dive bomber skims over an artillery emplacement. The swastika banner on the ground warns the pilot that this is a German position. "Stubborn Russian resistance had stopped our advance," noted Horn. "Stukas had to soften up the enemy positions."

October 17, 1941. Outside Borodino, a shell streaks from a camouflaged howitzer. "The village in front of us burns. I see something dark in the snow. It is the lieutenant. He is still warm, but I get no answer when I call his name. We have heard that Russian soldiers concentrate their fire at officers, who can be recognized by their slender, custom-made boots."

October 26, 1941. Stuck in the mud, the Germans lay tree trunks to build a corduroy road *(above, left)*. A horse-drawn cart hauling supplies to the laborers passes a captured rocket launcher *(above, right)*. "The work is exhausting," complained Horn, "the more so since we are extremely short of food. At night, we can see the searchlights and the flak firing around Moscow."

November 20, 1941. After resumption of the advance on roads finally frozen hard enough to support vehicles, a shell explodes in front of a forward observation tank—painted white to make it less visible against the snow. "The roads are icy and slippery, and the Russians fight with determination. In many places, exploding shells have blackened the snow."

November 28-29, 1941. A German truck *(left)* enters Istra—thirty miles from Moscow. "Istra is a small town with an impressive monastery, surrounded by a medieval wall with defensive towers. In the church, we see an antireligious exhibition in glass showcases. I photographed the magnificent gilded icons and the cupola *(below, right)* from the inside."

November 26, 1941. Sheltering in a barn, Horn's crew *(above)* uses a sheet-iron stove to cook a goat, the prize of a foraging expedition. "Plunder was severely punished in the German army, but if no owner was present, 'organizing' food was tolerated. The official ration was not enough for the hard work; it was only a watery soup, and bread was scarce."

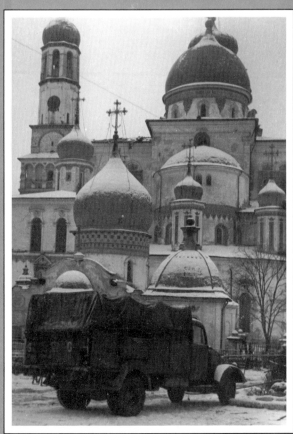

December 4, 1941. An 88 covers motorized infantry that had penetrated the outskirts of Moscow. "They pass us on the road back. All kinds of odd Russian clothing supplement their thin overcoats. The temperature is twenty below zero. Our socks freeze and stick to our boots."

December 8, 1941. At left below, a house burns after being torched by the Germans. Of those who lost their homes, Horn wrote: "When they suspect we will burn the houses, they run in and throw their buckets and pots out. These are their most important possessions."

December 8, 1941. "We join the long columns in retreat (below). It snows nearly without break. Cows are driven alongside for food. When Russian civilians try to join the column, we keep them back since we do not have enough food for them. We rest beside burned-down houses, close to the still-glowing beams. Our backs remain cold, but at least our fronts get warm."

February, 1942. Behind the lines stabilized by winter, a peasant *(left)* shows off her first-born child, and soldiers *(right)* prepare potatoes in a commandeered house. "The women get water daily," Horn observed, "two buckets from the village well. It is used mainly to cook the potatoes stored under the floor in their one room. Sleeping is done on the stove, which also serves as a source of heat."

April 27, 1942. Near Smolensk, the 10th Panzer prepares to leave Russia. "We rise at eight and start loading vehicles and guns on freight cars. We are assigned to a cattle car. During the wait until we leave, I chalk figures on the outside walls of our car. Two days later, we cross the border into East Prussia."

Trial by Fire and Ice

They had come to seize the Soviet capital, but on the bitter morning of December 5, 1941, the troops of Army Group Center were themselves in the grip of hostile elements. The blizzards of the past few days had relented, only to be replaced by some of the coldest weather the Germans had yet encountered. Before dawn, the temperature along the front fell to twenty-five degrees below zero. One regiment on the march during the night suffered 300 cases of frostbite. Shelter was at a premium, and soldiers huddled by the dozens in huts or dugouts, wearing every layer of lice-infested clothing they had brought with them from Germany or had scavenged since. Tentatively in the gray dawn, men began to stir, stamping their feet and chafing their hands around flickering camp stoves. Aided by sips of gritty ersatz coffee, members of the panzer corps stubbornly cranked up for action. But it would take more than will power to start their tanks and trucks, many of which had stalled for lack of sufficient antifreeze or cold-weather lubricants. For the moment, Adolf Hitler's mechanized vanguard was no more maneuverable than the ill-fated army of Napoléon that had plodded toward Moscow in 1812.

Not far to the east, meanwhile, Stalin's resilient war machine was in high gear. For weeks, fresh Red Army troops and supplies had arrived at the front on trains pulled by insulated locomotives, which were able to hold steam while their German counterparts choked in the cold. The Soviets had amassed roughly 700 tanks to face the battered panzers of Army Group Center; all of the Russian armored vehicles had been winterized, and many were equipped with compressed-air starters that worked in the deepest of freezes. To make headway where the terrain was too rough or heavily forested for tanks, the defenders of Moscow had twenty-two divisions of horse cavalry—a seeming anachronism that would prove timely in the primitive rigors of this campaign. And among the seventy-eight Russian rifle divisions guarding the capital were a number of ski battalions whose elusive riflemen, garbed in hard-to-see white, stood ready to exploit gaps in the overextended German line. Since late November, the resurgent Soviets had been flexing their muscle around Moscow, launching sporadic

Encrusted with snow, a German soldier endures sub-zero temperatures on the Russian front. "It is the Führer's express order that we hold out," General Adolf Strauss, commander of the Ninth Army, told a complaining subordinate. "There is no other way than to hold on, or die."

assaults that set the Germans back on their heels. Encouraged by these forays, Stalin and his staff prepared a campaign to drive the invaders away from the city. They would concentrate their attacks against the two armored pincers menacing Moscow—Heinz Guderian's Second Panzer Army to the south and Panzer Groups 3 and 4 to the north, under Georg-Hans Reinhardt and Erich Hoepner, respectively *(map, page 151)*. Hoepner's panzer vanguard—advancing to the right of Reinhardt's—stood within twenty miles of Moscow. But such progress was now a liability, for the panzers lacked the manpower to defend the salients they had forged.

The Soviets aimed the first blow of the counteroffensive at Reinhardt's left flank, south of the occupied city of Kalinin, and it descended while the German troops were emerging from their icy stupor on the morning of December 5. Heralded by the unearthly howl of Katyusha rockets, which raised plumes of snow as they hit and sent hot steel spewing in every direction, troops of General Ivan Konev's Kalinin Front surged across the frozen Volga River and attacked the invaders holed up on the west bank. Like figures in a nightmare, Germans fumbled for their rifles and machine guns, only to find some of the weapons useless because the oil had congealed overnight, clogging the moving parts. The attackers, by contrast, carried firearms that had been properly lubricated for such conditions. When they came up against pockets of resistance in the occupied villages, they had little difficulty outflanking them. Through the day, fast-moving Soviet ski troops probed for openings, engaging in firefights when necessary to clear a path, then pushing ahead through thick woods and over frozen marshes deep into enemy territory—effectively mimicking the Germans' own blitzkrieg tactics.

The following day, December 6, the pressure on the panzers increased as General Georgy Zhukov's formidable West Front joined in the counteroffensive to the south. That evening, Hoepner received permission from army group headquarters to pull back the exposed elements of his Panzer Group 4—a withdrawal that proceeded in good order, although much heavy equipment had to be abandoned along the way. The situation of Panzer Group 3, however, was growing more desperate by the hour. By December 7, Reinhardt's left flank had caved in, and Russian troops were bearing down on the only escape route open to his panzers—a road leading westward from the vital junction at Klin, a city roughly midway between Kalinin and Moscow.

A few miles to the north of Klin, Lieut. General Ferdinand Schaal, commander of the LVI Panzer Corps, was trying to organize resistance to strong Soviet probes against his left when Soviet infantry attacked his headquarters around midday. Unfazed, Schaal took up a rifle and fired back from

Soviet ski troops tow machine guns on sleds to augment their firepower during the December counteroffensive. The Russians had learned the value of highly mobile ski companies two years earlier in a war with Finland.

behind a truck. An unlikely coalition of staff officers, clerks, messengers, a few artillery and machine-gun sections, and a handful of self-propelled 20-mm antiaircraft guns joined in the fight and drove off the attackers. When Soviet armor arrived to lead a second assault, Schaal faced disaster until a number of tanks of the 25th Panzer Regiment came to the rescue. Resourceful mechanics had managed to start them by lighting fires under them. Bolstered by the reinforcements, Schaal repulsed the Soviets again, then prudently withdrew his command center to Klin. There he concentrated all available forces in a line that shielded the city's eastern flank, then veered westward just north of the town to protect the escape route. The panzer front was bending, but it refused to break.

Farther south, Guderian, too, was trying to extricate his forces from a perilous situation. Late on December 5, before the Soviets attacked in his sector, Guderian had concluded that his panzer army—which was packed into a slender salient jutting northeastward from the contested city of Tula—could not maintain its position and would have to pull back. For a general honored for his swift and relentless advances on two fronts, it was a painful concession. "This was the first time during the war that I had to make a decision of this sort," he noted later, "and none was more difficult." When Guderian gave notice of his intentions that evening to Field Marshal Fedor von Bock, the commander of Army Group Center, Bock inquired whether Guderian was close enough to the front lines to make such a determination. The suggestion riled the prickly Guderian, who prided himself on leading from the front. Losing touch with his vanguard "was one mistake that no panzer general ever made," he insisted. "I was close enough to the battle and to my soldiers to form a clear judgment of both."

Guderian's withdrawal was barely under way when Soviet troops attacked his vulnerable salient from all sides. Fierce fighting developed around Tula, which the Soviets used as a base to strike at the Germans as they funneled out of a trap of their own devising. "The Russians are pursuing us closely, and we must expect misfortunes to occur," Guderian wrote on December 8. His worries extended beyond the fate of his own army: If the Soviets sustained their momentum, they might drive through the heart of the invasion force and push the Wehrmacht against the borders of the Reich. As Guderian remarked ominously, "I am not thinking about myself but about our Germany. That is why I am frightened."

The threat to Army Group Center came at a fateful juncture in the career of Adolf Hitler. As the grim reports from the front poured into his East Prussian headquarters on December 6, Hitler maintained a confident air. He would not even contemplate a wholesale withdrawal around Moscow, reminding his aides that "the Russians never gave up anything of their own accord, and neither should we." If Hitler refused to admit the peril to Army Group Center, however, he was unable to ignore the danger facing the vanguard of Army Group North, which was on the verge of being surrounded at Tikhvin, east of Leningrad. On Sunday, December 7, he grudgingly authorized Field Marshal Wilhelm Ritter von Leeb to pull his exposed forces there back toward Leningrad, although he specified that Tikhvin's rail arteries were to be kept within artillery range—a condition that Leeb's hard-pressed units could not meet. Then, late that same Sunday, momentous news reached Wolfsschanze: Germany's ally Japan had entered the world war with a vengeance, attacking American forces at Pearl Harbor and the Philippines and the British at Malaya.

Ironically, Hitler had had less time than his counterpart in the Kremlin to prepare himself for such a turn of events. Thanks to the efforts of a Soviet double agent named Richard Sorge, who worked as a correspondent for a German newspaper and had penetrated both the German embassy in Tokyo and the Japanese cabinet there, Stalin had known for months that

Repulse at Moscow's Gates

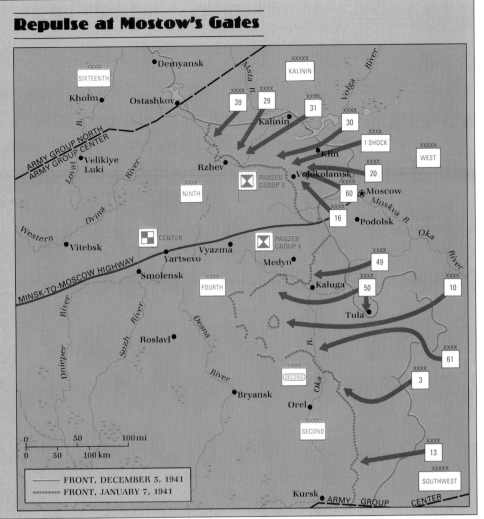

By early December, Army Group Center had lost its punch and was holding a vulnerable line (*solid red*) with two bulges—one north of Moscow, defended by Panzer Groups 3 and 4; the other south of the capital, held by the Second Panzer Army. Red Army troops attacked the salients on December 5 and 6 and drove the panzers back. The Russians then pressed their advantage along the line, engaging the three main bodies of German infantry. On December 8, they breached the thin Second Army line near Yelets and by the middle of the month had made similar gains against the Fourth Army in the center and the Ninth Army in the north. On December 16, Hitler tried to shore up the retracted German line by ordering his troops to stand fast. But Stalin committed fresh forces at either flank, and by early January, the Soviets had advanced farther (*dotted red line*). They were poised to break through around Rzhev in the north and Yukhnov in the south. From there, they could close their pincers on the Germans at Vyazma.

Japan would direct its war effort away from the Soviet Union and toward southeast Asia—intelligence that had encouraged him to transfer some of his best Siberian divisions to the defense of Moscow. Hitler, meanwhile, had clung to a slender hope that Japan would break its recent neutrality pact with Moscow and attack the Soviets. Not until late November did he receive a clear signal from Japan that its war aims lay elsewhere. Nonetheless, he professed to be delighted with his ally's bold stroke. "We cannot lose the war," he assured an associate. "Now we have a partner who has not been defeated in 3,000 years."

Technically, Hitler was not obliged to join his Asian partner in declaring war on the United States, for the Tripartite Pact that bound Germany, Italy, and Japan contained no specific military provisions. Hitler's foreign minister, Joachim von Ribbentrop, had offered verbal assurances that Germany would stand with Japan in any conflict with the United States, and a treaty had been drafted to that effect. But the treaty had yet to be signed when the Japanese launched their attacks, and Tokyo feared Hitler would insist that the Japanese join the campaign against the Soviets before he committed himself against the Americans.

Hitler, however, was in no mood to quibble with the Japanese in the aftermath of Pearl Harbor. His overriding concern was that Franklin D. Roosevelt would soon declare war on Germany, and he was determined to

151

beat the American president to the punch. Late on December 8, he boarded a train for Berlin, and three days later he declared war against the United States before the Reichstag. "We will always strike first," he assured the cheering deputies as he added the United States to Germany's growing list of enemies. "We will always deal the first blow!" In a remarkable diatribe, Hitler linked Roosevelt to the supposed Jewish conspiracy that the Führer regarded as the driving force behind the bolshevik regime in the east and the hostile democracies in the west. As Hitler saw it, Roosevelt had led America into war to divert attention from the failure of his domestic policies. "He was strengthened in this by the Jews around him," the Führer asserted. "The full diabolical meanness of Jewry rallied around this man, and he stretched out his hands."

As this tirade revealed, Hitler's racial obsessions increasingly warped his global vision. Indeed, those obsessions had already embroiled German military and occupation forces in atrocities against civilians on a vast scale. There could be no question of the Nazi regime ever coming to terms with

A Soviet officer rallies civilians around the bodies of Russian men and women hanged by the Germans to punish partisan activity in Volokolamsk, a city reclaimed by the Red Army in December. By initiating such tactics, Hitler hoped to "stamp out the will to resist."

its enemies and subjecting itself to international scrutiny. Even as Hitler declared war on the United States, SS *Einsatzgruppen*, or mobile execution squads, were completing a murderous sweep through the territories taken over by the Wehrmacht since June. Triggered by Hitler's call for the elimination of the so-called Jewish-bolshevik intelligentsia in the east, this purge claimed the lives of a relatively small number of Communist party commissars and large numbers of Jews, few of whom harbored much affection for Stalin or his cohorts.

Ostensibly, the Wehrmacht was exempt from participating in the slaughter, but in fact, the army accepted administrative responsibility for the Einsatzgruppen and provided their transportation and supplies while the Central Security Office maintained operational control. Since the Einsatzgruppen operated close to the front lines, many army commanders were aware of their activities, and some assisted in rounding up suspects as a way of pacifying their sectors. According to SS documents, Generals Reinhardt and Hoepner were among those who cooperated with the execution squads in an effort to "comb out" occupied areas; the commander of Einsatzgruppe A, which butchered more than 100,000 Jews in the first four months of the campaign, observed that his relations with Hoepner were "very close, yes, almost cordial." Some Jews eluded the fast-moving SS death squads, only to fall victim later to military police who lumped inoffensive Jews together with dedicated partisans. One SS report asserted that by December, Army Group Center had executed 19,000 "partisans and criminals, that is, in the majority, Jews."

The battlefront reversals of early December might have caused Hitler and his aides to reconsider the wisdom of conducting a savage race war and a punishing military campaign simultaneously. The massacres could scarcely go unnoticed: In many places, the victims were herded away by the thousands in broad daylight and gunned down in huge pits. Even civilians who were indifferent to the plight of the Jews had reason to be fearful, for German forces were answering partisan attacks with sweeping reprisals against the populace. To steel men for these acts, Nazi propagandists reminded them that the Slavs were "subhumans," little better than the "antihuman" Jews. As a result, the Germans—initially viewed as liberators by many people—accumulated fresh enemies behind the lines even as the situation at the front deteriorated. Yet Hitler's only response was to tighten the rack a notch. On the day the Japanese entered the war, he added a fresh twist to the terror in the occupied zones when he secretly decreed that civilians who posed a threat to German security were to vanish into the "night and fog." The order empowered security forces to detain or eliminate virtually anyone who struck them as suspect.

If Hitler's ruthless ideological crusade in the east was to succeed, however, the troops at the front would have to hold the line. On December 8, before departing for Berlin, he issued a directive to the beleaguered generals of Army Group Center. He conceded belatedly that the severe winter weather and consequent supply difficulties required the troops around Moscow to abandon "all major offensive operations and go over to the defensive," but he would sanction no withdrawals unless fortified lines could be prepared close by as rallying points. Given the difficulty of erecting such lines across frozen and forested terrain, the exposed units at the front entertained few hopes of relief.

Hitler's directive did nothing to shore up the crumbling German line around Moscow. Many units were already falling back when the order came down, and commanders could do little to halt such retreats short of sacrificing their men to the enemy. Indeed, within a few days of issuing his order, Hitler was compelled to authorize limited tactical withdrawals to prevent exposed units that had dutifully held their ground from being cut off and annihilated. One such defiant contingent was General Schaal's rear guard, holding the crossroads near Klin. By skillfully deploying his remaining tanks and by calling on every able-bodied man—including the drum corps of the 25th Panzer's regimental band—Schaal bought time for the escape of the main body of Panzer Group 3 and for the evacuation of the sick and wounded. By December 13, however, Soviet shelling had set much of the town on fire, and Schaal's rear guard was on the verge of being encircled. Around noon of the next day, with the last of the wounded clear, Schaal withdrew his forces while the 1st Panzer Division held off the Soviets pressing from the north.

Schaal was gratified by the tenacity of his own troops, but he sensed that overall German discipline was beginning to crack. "More and more soldiers were making their own way west," he wrote, "without weapons, leading a calf on a rope, or drawing a sledge with potatoes behind them—just trudging westward with no one in command. Men killed by aerial bombardment were no longer buried." The mere fact of having to retreat seemed to unnerve soldiers who were accustomed to driving the enemy before them. "Supply units were in the grip of psychosis, almost of panic," Schaal observed, "probably because in the past they had only been used to headlong advance." In the confusion, the troops abandoned equipment of all kinds. Artillery was discarded as the horses needed to pull the guns died of hunger or exposure, and many of the tanks and trucks the Germans had kept going by idling the engines through the night ran out of fuel and were left by the roadside.

Shivering Germans (left), who have thrown down their weapons in surrender, face Soviet captors, who are bundled in fur against the cold.

Nor was the crisis confined to the armored groups. Three German infantry armies bolstered the eroding Moscow front—Adolf Strauss's Ninth Army on the far left, Günther Hans von Kluge's Fourth Army in the center, and Rudolf Schmidt's Second Army on the far right. By mid-December, the Ninth and Fourth Armies had come under intense pressure and threatened to crack at the next blow. The weight of the Soviet onslaught had already proved too great for the Second Army, which was splitting down the middle in a vain attempt to maintain contact with Army Group South while protecting the right flank of Army Group Center. On the eve of the Russian counteroffensive, Schmidt's army held a front 180 miles long—or nearly two miles for every company.

Assailing the thin cordon on December 8, Soviet tanks, followed by cavalry and ski troops, broke through between the 45th and 95th Infantry

Divisions near the town of Yelets. By December 10, the wedge was sixteen miles wide and fifty miles deep and pointed toward the critical rail junction of Orel. In desperation, the army high command transferred General Wilfred von Oven's 56th Division from the Second Panzer Army and sent it piecemeal into the gap. Caught in the avalanche, isolated German units held out desperately in huts or in weapon pits of hard-packed snow until they faced certain annihilation and had to fight their way out. One infantryman recalled his unit's harrowing escape

to the rear through territory that had been reclaimed by the Soviets: "Whenever we moved into a village in the evening, we first had to eject the Russians," he wrote. "And when we got ready to move again in the morning, their machine guns were already stuttering behind our backs. Our dead comrades, whom we could not take along, lined the roads together with the dead bodies of horses." One Second Army division—the 45th Infantry—clawed its way to safety on December 14 but left behind nearly all of its vehicles, half of its guns, and 400 dead.

The deep thrust toward Orel created a fresh crisis for Guderian, who had extricated his panzers from their vulnerable salient with the intention of aligning them with the left flank of the Second Army south of Tula. Now the Second Army was retreating all along its punctured front, and Guderian concluded that his armor would also have to retreat to avoid envelopment. On December 14, he drove all day through a blizzard to confer in the rear with the army commander in chief, Walther von Brauchitsch, who had arrived the day before to assess the damage. Mindful of Hitler's order that no withdrawals be made unless defenses were prepared, Guderian asked for permission to pull his Second Panzer Army back to the line formed by the Oka River, north of Orel; this had been Guderian's front line in October and was thus partially fortified. At the conclusion of the meeting, Guderian received joint command of the Second Army and Second Panzer Army to coordinate their movements, and he thought he had persuaded Brauchitsch to let him pull both armies back to the October line, if necessary. But swaying Brauchitsch—derided by critics as little more than Hitler's postman—was one thing, and convincing the Führer was another.

In fact, Hitler had so little confidence in Brauchitsch that he had dispatched a trusted adjutant, Major General Rudolf Schmundt, to sit in on the conferences at the front and relay reports. As Hitler learned to his dismay, Guderian was just one of the field commanders urging a deep withdrawal. To the north, General Strauss had concluded that his Ninth Army could no longer hold Kalinin, the cornerstone in the army group's defenses above Moscow. A collapse there might doom Panzer Groups 3 and 4 unless they continued to fall back. Weighing the risks to his army group, Field Marshal Bock informed a sympathetic Brauchitsch that his forces would have to retreat en masse to the more defensible line—code-named the Königsberg Line, or K-Line—close to positions they had occupied in October, running southward from Rzhev past Orel to Kursk. Assuming that the troops could execute a withdrawal of fifty miles through snow and ice without being overrun by the swarming Soviets, the maneuver would ease Bock's critical supply situation and might leave Army Group Center in a position to renew the offensive in the spring.

Hitler, however, had long contended that will power was the decisive factor in conflicts between men and between nations. His own improbable triumph over adversity in his political battles seemed to confirm the point. Whatever the cost, the German army would have to prove its will in this crisis and root out the contagion of defeatism. To that end, Hitler overrode Bock and Brauchitsch and issued a new directive on December 16 that forbade even limited withdrawals. In plain terms, Hitler enjoined commanders "to intervene in person to compel the troops to fanatical resistance in their positions without regard to enemy breakthroughs on the flanks or in the rear."

To reinforce his hard line, Hitler shook up the command structure, placing Bock on leave—ostensibly for reasons of health—and naming the Fourth Army's chief, Kluge, to lead Army Group Center in Bock's stead. Ironically, Kluge had been criticized for failing to prod his Fourth Army forward in the waning stages of the Moscow offensive, but Hitler was confident that Clever Hans would faithfully uphold the stand-fast policy and turn a deaf ear to subordinates who sought to spare their units by retreating. If there were any lingering doubts as to who was in charge, Hitler dispelled them on December 19, when he accepted the resignation of Brauchitsch and assumed full responsibility for operations on the eastern front. Hitler blithely dismissed the complexity of the task he was taking on, assuring Franz Halder, chief of the army high command, that "this little affair of operational command is something anybody could do."

When the Führer's no-retreat order reached the front, it relieved some of the uncertainty plaguing the troops, who were dismayed by the mixed

signals they had been receiving. In the Fourth Army sector, orders to withdraw had been issued, countermanded, reinstated, and then rescinded again; in one area, engineers had laid and removed demolition charges on bridges three times in one day. After such fence-straddling, those who were not already in retreat welcomed a decision from the top, whatever hardships it entailed. Few soldiers who had shelter from the cold relished the thought of a long journey to the rear along icy roads; they knew that the arctic wind was as deadly as the camouflaged enemy, who emerged with terrible suddenness from the swirling snow. And many troops had grown attached to their cramped dugouts and huts despite the foul atmosphere that prevailed there—a miasma one cooped-up soldier described as a mixture of "stale urine, excrement, suppurating wounds, Russian tobacco, and the not-unpleasant smell of Kascha, a sort of buckwheat porridge." However pungent, such close quarters harbored the conditions of survival, and soldiers were prepared to fight for each fetid hovel as though it were their ancestral hearth.

While the Germans hunkered down, their adversaries grew bolder. By the middle of the month, Stalin felt confident that Moscow was indeed safe, and he recalled to the Kremlin many of the administrators and Politburo members who had been evacuated earlier in the year. He then committed fresh forces to the counteroffensive, aiming to pinch off the core of Army Group Center in a double envelopment like the one the Germans had executed with devastating effect earlier in the campaign. Under this plan,

Sabers raised, Soviet cavalrymen attack at a gallop during the winter campaign. Such headlong charges were the hallmark of the Cossacks, fierce horsemen who fought valiantly for the Red Army, yet resented Stalinist rule. In time, some Cossacks switched over to the German side.

the Soviets would increase the pressure on either German flank, pouring in reinforcements until two pincers converged in the vicinity of Vyazma, along the main highway from Moscow to Smolensk.

On the southern flank, the Germans were in no condition to counter the stepped-up attacks. Many panzer and infantry units were in full retreat when Hitler's stand-fast directive reached them, and they had no established positions to hold or shelters to defend. On December 18, an exasperated Guderian received specific instructions from Hitler to hold ground that his men had already conceded. Convinced that Hitler and his aides failed to appreciate the gravity of the situation, Guderian decided to appeal to the Führer directly for permission to complete the withdrawal of his forces to the October line. On December 20, the panzer leader boarded a plane for Wolfsschanze, embarking on what he later described as a "long flight from the icebound battle area north of Orel to the well-appointed and well-heated supreme headquarters far away in East Prussia."

As a pioneer of the blitzkrieg concept, Guderian had long been in Hitler's good graces, but when he arrived at the Wolf's Lair he saw in the Führer's eyes "for the first time a hard, unfriendly expression." The conference soon took on a tone to match. When Hitler insisted that Guderian's men "dig into the ground where they are and hold every square yard of land," Guderian pointed out that the ground was frozen to a depth of five feet and impervious to "our wretched entrenching tools." Hitler then suggested that the troops use howitzers to blast defensive craters, as the Germans had done in World War I. Guderian observed that even if he were to expend his precious shells to that end, they would yield only "hollows in the ground, each about the width and depth of a washtub."

His tactical arguments rebuffed, Hitler fell back on his authority as supreme leader, insisting that he was entitled to ask "any German soldier to lay down his life." Guderian countered that "such a sacrifice may be asked of a man only if the results to be obtained are worth having." He then made one last effort to win Hitler's approval for the withdrawal, pointing out that the October line offered some protection against the weather as well as the Soviets. "We are suffering twice as many casualties from the cold as from the fire of the Russians," he argued. "Anyone who has seen the hospitals filled with frostbite cases must realize what that means." The Führer, however, would not be moved. He advised Guderian to pay less attention to the suffering of his troops: "You feel too much pity for them. You should stand back more."

Guderian would soon have an opportunity to take a longer view of the events at the front. He returned to find an old nemesis, Kluge, in command of Army Group Center. Several days later, the town of Chern fell to Soviets who poured through a gap they had punched between the Fourth Army and the Second Panzer Army. Guderian and Kluge argued violently over who was responsible for losing the position, and Guderian threatened to resign. To his chagrin, the next day Guderian was relieved of command by order of the Führer. Kluge had persuaded Hitler to act on the grounds that Guderian, though a fine commander, lacked discipline.

To the north, Hitler's stand-fast order was having more effect. By December 19, Panzer Groups 3 and 4 had stopped retreating and were holding a line above the Moscow-to-Vyazma highway, roughly midway between those two cities. Along the highway, troops of the Fourth Army were completing a harrowing withdrawal; Cossacks of the II Guards Cavalry Corps, led by Major General L. M. Dovator, had dogged them every step of the way. The general, on horseback, always rode near the front, driving his troopers to strike at the retreating Germans. Dovator did not relent even when the last panzers crossed the Ruza River, whose frozen expanse offered German machine gunners of the 252d Infantry Division on the west bank a clear field of fire. On the morning of December 19, Dovator sent his vanguard dismounted across the Ruza. German gunners shattered the attack and pinned down the surviving Cossacks on the ice. Determined to direct the survivors' escape, the general handed the reins of his horse to his groom, cocked his pistol, and courageously strode down to the east bank of the river. As he stepped onto the ice, a machine gun stuttered on the far bank and Dovator toppled into a drift of snow. Several aides ran to his side, and they, too, were cut down. The Cossacks fell back, dragging the lifeless body of their general with them. For the moment at least, the center of the German line was holding.

The army group faced a bleaker prospect on the far left, in Adolf Strauss's Ninth Army sector. As Strauss feared, the Soviets had taken Kalinin on December 16, and in the days that followed they stepped up the pressure, determined to break through to Rzhev and thence to Vyazma. In conjunction with his stand-fast order, Hitler insisted that the Fourth Army hold the line at Staritsa, thirty miles northeast of Rzhev. Strauss balked at the command, aware that the Staritsa line was an arbitrary designation and presented no natural obstacles to the enemy. Like Guderian, Strauss wanted to withdraw to the front that his men had held in October—behind the Volga River, running through Rzhev. But when he flew to Smolensk on December 21 to plead his case with the new commander of Army Group Center, Field Marshal Kluge, he came up against a stone wall. Kluge assured Strauss that his army was in an excellent position and sent him back to the front to do the Führer's bidding.

It was a cheerless yuletide for the men of the Ninth Army. Holiday parcels from home and bundles of winter clothing did not arrive at the railway station near Staritsa until after Christmas, and before the precious goods could be distributed, Soviet raiders broke through and set the depot afire. All that was salvaged was a shipment of Swiss cheese, which ravenous German soldiers carved up with bayonets and wolfed down without ceremony. By New Year's Eve, the line that Hitler had ordered Strauss to hold had been shredded. Here and there, German units were defending villages in hedgehog fashion—prepared for attack from every side—as the enemy nipped at their flanks and menaced their rear. The lonely struggle in the cold was beginning to tell on German morale. One of Strauss's subordinates reported that his division had been reduced to regiment strength and was surrounded by ski troops. "The men are just dropping with fatigue," he described. "They flop into the snow and die from exhaustion. What they are expected to do is sheer suicide. The young soldiers are turning on their officers, screaming at them: 'Why don't you just go ahead and kill us? It makes no difference who does us in.'"

As the new year dawned, even Kluge counseled Hitler to reconsider the threat to Army Group Center and allow a wholesale withdrawal. To be sure, Panzer Groups 3 and 4 were still holding the line north of the highway—a fact that Hitler acknowledged by promoting them to the status of panzer armies even though they had been reduced in recent weeks to roughly corps strength. But south of the highway, in the Fourth Army's rear, Russian troops who had broken through at Chern on Christmas Day were advancing toward the supply depots at Yukhnov and Sukhinichi, scarcely fifty miles from Vyazma. German administrative and reinforcement battalions hurriedly fortified the towns and braced for the onslaught. To the north, where Hitler had staked so much on the defense of the Staritsa line, the attackers were on the verge of a major breakthrough. The "little business" of operational command that the Führer had assumed grew more agonizing by the day. And the dilemma of Army Group Center was only part of Hitler's problem: At the southernmost tip of the invasion front, on the shore of the Black Sea, another German army was caught in a cauldron.

The crisis facing the Wehrmacht in the Crimea stemmed from decisions taken independently by the German and Soviet high commands shortly after the counteroffensive around Moscow had begun. Although his troops were on the defensive there and around Leningrad, Hitler had ordered Army Group South to reclaim the initiative for the Reich and, when weather allowed, to retake Rostov and the Donets Basin. The group was also to capture Sevastopol, the principal Russian navy base on the Black Sea and the only part of the Crimea still in Soviet hands. The Sevastopol mission fell to Erich von Manstein's Eleventh Army, which would have to reduce the heavily fortified port while guarding the vulnerable Kerch Peninsula to the east—a spit of land separated from the Soviet-held Caucasus by a strait less than two miles wide in some places (map, next page). Aware that Sevastopol could not be taken by half measures, Manstein committed six of his seven divisions to the attack, leaving the 46th Infantry Division—10,000 men—and a few inferior Rumanian brigades to cover the peninsula.

Unbeknown to Manstein, the Soviets were plotting a coup of their own—an amphibious assault on the peninsula to be mounted by more than 40,000 troops. Moscow ordered the attack on December 7, but preparations took more than two weeks. Before the Soviets moved, Manstein's troops attacked Sevastopol. Advancing under cover of an earthshaking artillery barrage, the Germans broke through the port's outer ring of fortifications on December 17. Ahead, two more cordons girded the city and its strategic harbor on the Bay of Sevastopol.

The main German thrust came just north of Sevastopol, where Manstein hoped to punch through to the bay and bring LIV Corps's heavy artillery close enough to prevent the Soviet navy from relieving the besieged port. But even with powerful support from the Luftwaffe—operating effectively in weather that was benign compared with the forbidding conditions that hobbled pilots and ground crews farther north—the troops made only halting progress across hilly terrain. When the assault battalions came up against the defenders' stout earth-and-timber dugouts, they had to root out

As his forces retreated near Moscow and Leningrad, Hitler ordered Erich von Manstein's Eleventh Army, in the Crimea, to storm Sevastopol. The attack, launched December 17, met stiff resistance and was suspended after Russian troops landed on the nearby Kerch Peninsula. In bitter fighting, the Germans contained the Russians on the peninsula. Encouraged by Soviet gains, Stalin mounted an offensive all along the front in early January. Although Army Group Center remained the principal Soviet target, the Red Army opened fresh gaps elsewhere in the German line. North of Lake Ilmen, shock troops smashed through the Eighteenth Army and headed for besieged Leningrad before foundering in the snow. South of the lake, the attackers trapped much of the Sixteenth Army in a massive pocket at Demyansk and a smaller one at Kholm. Army Group South, meanwhile, responded to a breakthrough around Izyum and had contained the threat by early February.

Breakthroughs All Along the Front

Gulf of Finland

FRONT, EARLY JANUARY 1942
FRONT, LATE FEBRUARY 1942
SOVIET DEFENSES OF SEVASTOPOL

Leningrad — LENINGRAD — XXXX
EIGHTEENTH — XXXX

59 — XXXX
VOLKHOV — XXXXX
2 SHOCK
52 — XXXX
11 — XXXX
34 — XXXX
NORTHWEST — XXXXX

Demyansk
3 SHOCK — XXXX
Kholm
4 SHOCK — XXXX
Ostashkov
22 — XXXX
KALININ — XXXXX
Kalinin
31 — XXXX
30 — XXXX
Dmitrov

ARMY GROUP NORTH
ARMY GP. CENTER
Velikiye Luki
Rzhev
NINTH — XXXX
1 SHOCK — XXXX
Moscow — WEST — XXXXX
Volokolamsk
5 — XXXX
33 — XXXX
Podolsk
43 — XXXX

THIRD — XXXX
Vitebsk
Yartsevo
39 — XXXX
FOURTH — XXXX
Vyazma
Medyn
49 — XXXX
50 — XXXX
Tula

CENTER
IV AIRBORNE CORPS (PART)
Smolensk
FOURTH — XXXX
Dorogobuzh
Kaluga
10 — XXXX

Borisov
Mogilev
Roslavl
61 — XXXX

Minsk
Zukovka

BELORUSSIA

SOVIET UNION

PRIPET MARSHES
Pripet River
Bryansk
SECOND — XXXX
Orel
Kromy
BRYANSK — XXXXX
SECOND — XXXX

Chernigov
Seim R. — Kursk
ARMY GROUP CENTER
ARMY GROUP SOUTH
Voronezh

Konotop
Krasnoye
SIXTH — XXXX
Belgorod
Volchansk
SOUTHWEST — XXXXX

Kiev
Mirgorod
SOUTH
Kharkov
Don River
6 — XXXX
57 — XXXX

UKRAINE

Cherkassy
Poltava
Krasnograd
Izyum
Donets River

Dnepropetrovsk
SEVENTEENTH — XXXX
Voroshilovgrad
SOUTH — XXXXX

Zaporozhe
Stalino
Taganrog
Rostov

THIRD RUMANIAN — XXXX
Mariupol
Mius R.

Melitopol

Kherson
SEA OF AZOV
TRANSCAUCASUS — XXXXX

RUMANIA

Odessa
CRIMEA — XXXXX

CRIMEA
Kerch
51 — XXXX
ELEVENTH — XXXX
Feodosiya
44 — XXXX

Sevastopol
BLACK SEA

0   50   100   150 mi
0   50 100 150 km

the Russians at considerable cost. After five grueling days, the 22d Infantry Division—Manstein's vanguard north of Sevastopol—had fought through the second defensive line and was bearing down on the third, within sight of the harbor. Then Soviet reinforcements struck back, supported by shellfire from warships offshore and massive coastal guns in Sevastopol, and stopped the Germans in their tracks.

The contest was still at issue on December 26, when Manstein learned that Russian troops were coming ashore on the Kerch Peninsula. Aggressive as ever, Manstein refused to abandon the assault on Sevastopol, ordering his forward units north of the port to redouble their efforts to reach the bay. The 16th Infantry Regiment of the 22d Division eventually penetrated Fort Stalin—a lofty bastion on Sevastopol's inner perimeter offering a sweeping view of the harbor. Then, however, the attack faltered. Manstein's vanguard was too worn out to exploit the breakthrough, and a deteriorating situation on the peninsula left him no choice but to send reinforcements eastward.

Until help arrived, the Kerch Peninsula was defended by the 46th Infantry Division, led by Lieut. General Hans von Sponeck, a Prussian count who had earned the Knight's Cross of the Iron Cross commanding airborne troops in Holland. At first, Sponeck's troops proved more than equal to the task. The oncoming Soviets lacked proper landing craft and naval support. They waded ashore up to the neck in frigid waters, bringing neither artillery nor vehicles with them. Their first beachheads, around the port of Kerch, were narrow and scattered; the Germans sealed them off with ease.

Late on December 28, however, an ominous new threat developed. That night, 5,000 Russians came ashore at the Black Sea port of Feodosiya, at the western end of the Kerch Peninsula, where a single German battalion, the 46th Engineers, stood in their way. Sponeck moved to contain the beachhead, but on receiving a mistaken report that still another landing was under way north of Feodosiya, on the Sea of Azov, he concluded that the 46th Division would soon be trapped on the peninsula. He ordered it to retreat at once to the Crimean mainland. When Manstein learned of the order, he tried to countermand it, but he had lost radio contact with Sponeck's headquarters and the withdrawal continued. Frigid air had descended on the Crimea from the north, and the men of the 46th trudged westward in a scene much like the humiliations recently visited on the Germans outside Moscow and Leningrad—ghostly figures limping through sleet and snow, cheeks waxy with frostbite, leaving their frozen dead by the wayside along with stalled trucks and gun carriages and the emaciated carcasses of draft horses.

Quick work by the Soviets at Feodosiya might have shut the escape route

A Russian civilian comforts his wife near the remains of their son, one of many partisans shot by the Germans before they withdrew from the eastern Crimea.

of the 46th Division and imperiled Manstein's entire position, but the commanders of the Russian force showed little initiative. On the morning of December 30, the 46th Engineer Battalion still held out in Feodosiya. Far from contemplating withdrawal, its commander was trying to persuade a Rumanian cavalry brigade that had linked up with the Germans during the night to join them in a counterattack. When the Rumanian commander finally declined, the engineers went it alone in a snowstorm, only to come up against a rude surprise—Soviet tanks, freshly unloaded from ships docked at the seaport. The Germans took aim with their few 37-mm antitank guns, but ice had formed in the breeches and the weapons failed to fire. Galvanized by the impetuous attack, the Soviets drove their opponents from Feodosiya and advanced several miles to the north, but they failed to reach the Sea of Azov, and on December 31, the haggard men of the 46th filed through the opening.

The days that followed were agonizing for Manstein. He managed to halt the demoralized 46th Division just west of the peninsula and drew up a defensive cordon with the help of the reinforcements from Sevastopol. Nonetheless, the entire Kerch Peninsula had become a Soviet staging ground, and Manstein feared for his army. On January 4, a fresh threat materialized at Yevpatoriya, a Black Sea port forty miles north of Sevastopol. Soviet troops stormed ashore and, with the help of paratroopers and a partisan uprising in the town, forged a sizable bridgehead. An infantry regiment alertly dispatched by Manstein reached the scene, however, and ousted the Soviets after three days of hard fighting. Manstein followed up this success by driving the Russians from Feodosiya, but his army was unable to retake the peninsula. A nervous calm settled over the Crimea as the two sides regrouped, eyeing each other warily across the Kerch line and the shell-pocked perimeter at Sevastopol.

The loss of the Kerch Peninsula infuriated Hitler. He had looked to his Crimean army for a coup, only to be presented with another debacle. He found a scapegoat in the person of General Sponeck, whose unauthorized withdrawal had plainly violated the Führer's stand-fast order. Sponeck had considered it his first duty to extricate his men from a position he deemed untenable—a view consistent with the strict but gentlemanly Prussian military tradition that Hitler detested. The Führer insisted that his commanders abandon all scruples and approach the war in the east as a struggle to the death. To that end, he had Sponeck recalled from the front and court-martialed by a special tribunal headed by Reich Marshal Hermann Göring. The court stripped Sponeck of his rank and decorations and sentenced him to die. At Manstein's request, Hitler stayed the execution and later commuted the sentence to seven years in prison. Yet the message

Combatants who served at least fourteen days on the Russian front between November 1941 and April 1942 received this decoration, which is inscribed, "Winter Battle in the East."

was clear: Commanders who defied the Führer to spare their men did so at the risk of their reputations, if not their lives.

While Hitler rang in the new year with recriminations, Stalin drew up a long list of military resolutions for the months ahead. Confident now to the point of recklessness, the Soviet leader wanted to expand the campaign dramatically and repulse the Germans all along the front. On January 5, he put the proposal before several of his top aides, including General Zhukov. Like the cavalryman he used to be, Zhukov attacked the idea head-on, arguing forcefully that all available Soviet reserves should be concentrated against Army Group Center, the weakest link in the German chain. Inspired by this rare show of independent thinking within the Kremlin, Stalin's chief of war production, Nikolai Voznesenskiy, backed up Zhukov, pointing out that a general offensive might soon exhaust the nation's limited supply of weapons and ammunition. Since June, many Soviet arms plants in the Germans' path had been relocated to central and eastern Russia; entire factories had been stripped down, carted off, and reassembled. It would take time for the nation's war industries to regain their footing. Stalin, however, was deaf to such objections. Like Hitler, he regarded his aides as mere instruments of his will, and he closed the debate with an injunction that brooked no appeal: At every vulnerable point along the extended front, he insisted, "we must pound the Germans to pieces so they won't be able to mount an offensive in the spring."

The Russian offensive would test the limits of the Red Army's tactical skills as well as its material reserves. Despite the emergence of a promising new generation of field commanders—most of them, like Zhukov, in their early forties—the Soviet officer corps was still recuperating from Stalin's ruinous purges of the late 1930s. Many commanders were hampered by inexperience and by a fear of failure that stymied initiative. To make matters worse, the opening months of the campaign had conditioned the army to think defensively. With the exception of the shock troops pounding Army Group Center, Soviet officers and men knew so little about offensive operations that the general staff felt compelled to spell out such rudiments as the need to concentrate forces at weak points in the enemy line and to punch through decisively "in a single direction."

What they lacked in polish, the Soviets made up for in numbers and determination. As Stalin's offensive unfolded, they subjected large elements of Army Groups North and South to the sort of pressure the Germans in the center had been enduring for more than a month. In the north, the Soviets attacked on either side of Lake Ilmen on January 7. The upper thrust was directed toward besieged Leningrad, the lower toward the vulnerable right flank of Army Group North, whose position had been undermined by the erosion of the left flank of Army Group Center. A breakthrough to the north of Lake Ilmen—a single wedge four miles wide—soon lost cohesion as the shock units fanned out across the wild, snow-covered terrain and faltered for lack of supplies and coordination. South of the lake, the attackers breached the enemy line at more than one point and moved effectively to envelop the Germans.

By January 12, Field Marshal Wilhelm Ritter von Leeb, concerned about the right flank of his army group, asked Hitler to sanction its withdrawal to the Lovat River, running southward through the city of Kholm. Predictably, Hitler rejected the request, whereupon Leeb asked to be relieved of command. The Führer complied, naming the commander of the Eighteenth Army, Lieut. General Georg von Kuechler, as Leeb's replacement. In the weeks ahead, Kuechler would have no choice but to assume a hedgehog defense south of Lake Ilmen as the Soviets encircled his front-line forces, leaving one major pocket of German resistance around the town of Demyansk and a smaller one at Kholm (pages 169-172).

In the south, Soviet troops surged across the Donets River on either side of the town of Izyum and tore a huge hole in the thin line of the German Seventeenth Army. The breakthrough came as a rude welcome for the new commander of Army Group South, Field Marshal Fedor von Bock, who had returned early from sick leave on January 18 to fill the gap left when Field Marshal Walther von Reichenau suffered a fatal stroke. Bock was anxious to make the most of this second chance—Hitler had restored him to prominence in order to allay public concern over the abrupt departure of so many notable German generals in recent weeks. It took Bock time to organize a response around Izyum, however, and by January 25, the attackers had forged a wedge that was fifty miles wide and nearly as deep. But again, the Soviets lost momentum as they cut deeper into German-held territory, hampered in part by the difficulty of maintaining supply lines in weather that grew nastier toward the end of the month. They were handicapped as well by the isolated nature of their thrust, which left Bock free to concentrate powerful forces around the bulge in a deft realignment. Dreadful mismatches resulted. On the last day of January, Soviet cavalrymen moving southwestward in a driving snowstorm outdistanced their supporting tanks and came up against armored units of Ewald von Kleist's First Panzer Army, whose gunners turned their turrets on the hapless horsemen and blasted them away.

Puzzled by the willingness of the Soviets to expend their resources in such scattershot fashion, Halder remarked that Stalin's sweeping offensive seemed to be "degenerating into a brawl." Indeed, the farther the Russians reached and the harder they flailed, the less they accomplished. The

The Indomitable Defenders of Kholm

Germans approach a dead Russian at Kholm. Above, Richard Muck's map outlines the German pocket.

The Soviets' massive counteroffensive in the winter of 1941-1942 isolated as many as 100,000 Germans in embattled pockets of resistance. One Wehrmacht detachment garrisoned Kholm, a strategically important town situated at the confluence of the Lovat and Kunya rivers *(map, above)* in the northern sector of the front. The 5,000 defenders of Kholm were surrounded by three Soviet divisions, a force roughly five times as large as their own.

Command of the seemingly futile German defense fell to Brigadier General Theodor Scherer. Combat Group Scherer was a motley collection of rear-echelon troops—supply units, military police, Luftwaffe and naval personnel, and soldiers from three infantry divisions, some of them newly arrived on the eastern front. His men had only a handful of mortars and antitank guns; they possessed neither tanks nor heavy artillery. To break up Russian assaults, the defenders relied on air support and radio-directed fire from German guns six miles outside the encircled perimeter.

Despite the odds, the garrison at Kholm heeded Adolf Hitler's injunction to offer "fanatical resistance." For three grim months of ceaseless combat, they held on, and when a German relief column finally broke through on May 5, it was greeted by 1,200 haggard survivors. The resolute defense had been chronicled by a German correspondent, Richard Muck. His photographs, shown here and on the following pages, were published in a book that provided stirring propaganda for the home front.

German soldiers brave Russian fire as they move through the battle-ravaged streets of Kholm *(above, left)*. In the course of the siege, the Germans were forced to yield half of their one-square-mile perimeter to superior Soviet numbers, but the attackers paid a price. "The Soviets buy each step with blood," correspondent Muck reported; "a mountain of dead bolshevists" fell to German machine guns and the 37-mm antitank gun at left.

The garrison of Kholm was sustained by a precarious aerial supply line. Canisters containing food, ammunition, and medical supplies were parachuted into a bullet-swept drop zone (*above*) that lay just outside the German lines. Although many canisters fell into Soviet hands, regular issues of bread, canned meat, and cigarettes bolstered the spirit of the defenders (*right*).

Following the relief of Kholm, a bearded General Scherer decorates one of his soldiers—a veteran of World War I—with the Iron Cross (left). Scherer, who had been wounded during the siege, was awarded the Knight's Cross for directing the defense.

At Hitler's order, a special badge called the Kholm Shield (below) was issued to the surviving defenders of Kholm. Thanks to their bravery and endurance, the city remained in German hands for another two years.

campaign was taking on a new complexion, and nowhere was the shift of greater consequence than in the teeming battleground west of Moscow, where Army Group Center was holding on for its life.

The opening of the Soviet general offensive had fundamentally changed the situation of Army Group Center. By the second week of January, Soviet objectives there were no longer limited to pinching off the Germans at Vyazma. That operation would proceed, but it would be accompanied by an outer envelopment directed toward Smolensk—85 miles west of Vyazma—designed to trap enemy elements that escaped before the inner ring closed. The ambitious plan reflected Stalin's rising optimism as well as his readiness to overlook the Red Army's deficiencies. To reach Smolensk, Soviet units would have to advance nearly 200 miles from their starting points while maintaining cohesion and preserving their tenuous supply lines. It was a long shot at best, and it would divert precious resources from an inner envelopment that was by no means assured.

While Stalin dreamed of a sweeping victory, Hitler slowly waked to the realities facing Army Group Center and allowed it some room to maneuver, even if that meant yielding ground. The concession came grudgingly. As late as January 8, Hitler had not hesitated to relieve General Hoepner when the commander sanctioned the withdrawal of a single corps whose flank had been turned by enemy troops advancing south of the Moscow-to-Vyazma highway. Yet that incursion was small when compared with the massive breaches the Soviets were opening around Rzhev in the north and between Sukhinichi and Yukhnov in the south. The Germans had feared a breakthrough at Rzhev since the Staritsa line gave way at year's end. Now the Russians were driving a wedge through the tired Ninth Army and isolating the battered Third and Fourth Panzer Armies north of the highway. And to the south, the Soviets were forging an equally dangerous gap between the Fourth Army and the Second Panzer Army, Guderian's former command. Try as he might, Hitler could not deny that his forces were being divided and, if they remained in place, would soon be conquered. On January 15, he authorized the step he had spent the past month resisting—a tactical withdrawal to the Königsberg Line.

It was a belated bow to reality. In some places, the Germans had already been pushed back beyond that line. And the order by no means eliminated the risk of envelopment: The K-Line crossed the main highway near Gzhatsk, thirty-five miles east of Vyazma. Yet Hitler's concession gave his field commanders the flexibility they sorely needed. Now, as the army group retrenched, forces could be spared for selective counterattacks to stop the dangerous gaps to the north and south.

To carry out that rigorous task in the north, Kluge made an inspired appointment: He named General Walter Model, leader of the XLI Panzer Corps, to replace the battle-worn General Strauss as commander of the Ninth Army. In appearance, Model was the model of a Prussian general—a stolid figure replete with monocle—but in action he was a restless dynamo, scouting the front lines in his reconnaissance aircraft and touching down at trouble spots to rally his troops in the fashion of Guderian and Erwin Rommel. Following a brief conference with Hitler, Model arrived at Ninth Army headquarters at Vyazma on January 18 and informed his staff that he would move at once to pinch off the Rzhev gap and grasp the Russians "in a stranglehold." His officers looked at him in mute astonishment until one of them plucked up the courage to ask, "And what, Herr General, have you brought us for this operation?" Model replied serenely, "Myself," then burst into a hearty laugh that broke the ice in the chilly staff room.

Model was as good as his word. Mustering all the strength his army could spare, he deployed the VI Corps, beefed up with heavy and light flak detachments, on the west side of the gap and the XXIII Corps on the east. On January 21, the 1st Panzer Division, now without tanks and fighting as infantry, attacked first from the town of Sychevka northward toward Rzhev. Model's forces, supported by Luftwaffe fighters and self-propelled assault guns, leaped into the breach on January 22. Caught indeed in Model's grasp, the surprised Soviets scattered or were crushed. In less than thirty-six hours, the converging German spearheads made contact, restoring the Ninth Army's front above Vyazma.

The situation below Vyazma remained precarious, however. The Fourth Army had fought hard to contain the enemy bulge to the south. But on January 26, a Russian cavalry corps under Major General P. A. Belov broke through the German screen near Yukhnov and surged north toward Vyazma. Belov's troopers were not the only imminent threat. Infantry units were making similar incursions from the east, and in recent days thousands of Soviet paratroopers had landed just south of the main highway and were menacing that German lifeline, which appeared doomed if the flow of Soviet troops and supplies from the southeast continued. But at month's end, in a maneuver similar to Model's bold counterthrust, the Fourth Panzer Army drove south from Gzhatsk and linked up with units of the Fourth Army above Yukhnov, shoring up the army group's line below the highway and giving the Germans defending the road through Vyazma the respite they needed to secure the artery.

Zhukov could only rue Stalin's decision to widen the campaign. One of Zhukov's strongest outfits—the First Shock Army—had already been transferred north to the vicinity of Demyansk, a decision that moved him to

Staving Off Annihilation

The deadliest thrusts of the Soviet attempt to smash Army Group Center in early 1942 were the pincers closing on the main highway at Vyazma. Russian troops pierced the Ninth Army line near Rzhev, and a massive Soviet penetration around Sukhinichi endangered Vyazma from the south. By January 14, Army Group Center's position had become so precarious that Hitler ordered a withdrawal to roughly the line his forces had held in October (*dashed red line*). Many German units remained subject to envelopment after this adjustment, but the move shortened the front, freeing units for counterattacks that sealed the worst gaps in the German line. Meanwhile, another Soviet wave swept from the north in a wide arc toward German-held Smolensk. But the great distances involved left the attackers spent before they reached their objective. By mid-February, the Germans were firmly planted along a convoluted line (*red dots*), with the Ninth Army out front, holding the Soviets at bay.

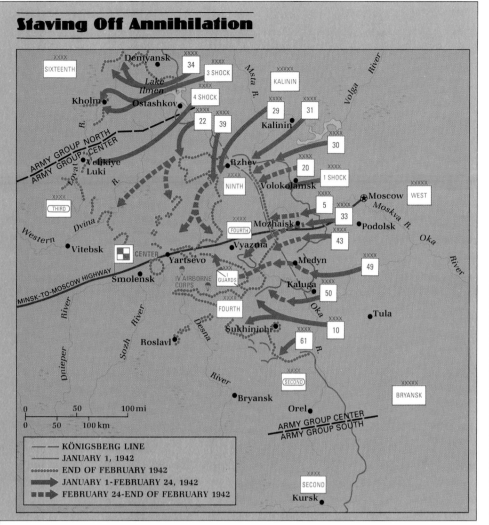

KÖNIGSBERG LINE
JANUARY 1, 1942
END OF FEBRUARY 1942
JANUARY 1-FEBRUARY 24, 1942
FEBRUARY 24-END OF FEBRUARY 1942

phone Stalin and complain, only to have the dictator hang up on him. With more troops and supplies, Zhukov might well have closed the ring at Vyazma. As it was, his most aggressive units were paying a fearful price as the Germans shut the door behind them. Given a decent meal, wrote a Soviet lieutenant, his men "would charge into a rain of bullets without batting an eyelid, but they are hungry. They are losing their strength."

To add to Zhukov's frustrations, the outer envelopment that was supposed to finish off Army Group Center at Smolensk was developing properly on only one flank. The plan called for the Bryansk Front, on Zhukov's left, to push through to Orel and turn northwestward to Smolensk. The Bryansk Front, however, was weak and undersupplied, and the Germans opposing it—forces that Guderian had stubbornly withdrawn in December—had profited from their rest and were holding steady. As a result, the projected double envelopment consisted of only a single wing—albeit a formidable one—in the north. Advancing through the yawning gap between Army Group North and Army Group Center south of Lake Ilmen, masses of Russian troops swept around the flank of Model's Ninth Army in late January and descended toward Smolensk before foundering in the face of stiff opposition and dwindling supplies.

The envelopment left the Ninth Army facing Soviets to the east, north, and west. As one of Model's officers remarked, it was the "strangest front the army ever had." Ringed by a virtual Red sea, the Ninth Army tenaciously held a peninsula that extended south from Rzhev to Gzhatsk. The Fourth Panzer Army, backed by the Fourth Army, defended the narrow passageway from Gzhatsk to Vyazma—which linked the Ninth Army peninsula to the main body of German-held territory. This enabled headquarters to withdraw the Third Panzer Army from the pocket and station it along the highway to the north of Smolensk to hold off the Russian vanguard sweeping down from the north.

It was the most precarious of lines. Concerted opposition could have shattered it in a fortnight. Yet the Soviets, like the Germans, were at the end of their tether—and the units that had ranged the farthest were the closest to snapping. Savage contests for small parcels of territory would continue west of Moscow into April, but, as Halder had observed, these were brawls more than battles. Army Group Center had weathered the storm.

As spring melted the snows along the front and slathered both sides in mud, the Germans counted their blessings and did what they could to relieve isolated forward units that had held out for months. The largest of these islands of resistance was at Demyansk, south of Lake Ilmen, where roughly 100,000 soldiers had been cut off. On February 22, Hitler designated Demyansk a fortress, ruling out any thought of surrender or a breakout. Holding the fortress into the spring was vital; the roads that met there would be essential to offensive operations in the area once the surrounding marshlands thawed. To supply the defenders, the Luftwaffe embarked on a huge airlift, flying a hundred transports into Demyansk each day in all kinds of weather. In two months, more than 60,000 tons of cargo was carried in and 35,000 wounded or exhausted troops ferried out. Despite the airlift, conditions inside the fortress worsened as the weeks passed. While haggard soldiers subsisted on the flesh of the garrison's diseased horses, Russian civilians waited outside the field kitchens to collect the entrails and bones. Not until late April did a German relief column slog through the mud from the west to open a corridor to Demyansk.

On April 26, a few days before Demyansk was relieved, Hitler announced before the Reichstag that the Wehrmacht had passed its terrible trial in Russia and was ready to move forward again. "A world struggle was decided during the winter," he insisted, contrasting his own persistence and Napoléon's retreat from Moscow in 1812: "We have mastered the destiny that broke another man 130 years ago." Yet in the same speech, the Führer indirectly conceded that the days of the blitzkrieg were done and that the war would continue for some time. He assured the deputies that the troops would be ready for the next winter, "no matter where it finds us."

A supply-laden Ju 52 touches down at besieged Fortress Demyansk in late winter 1942. The successful airlift—whose survivors were awarded the Demyansk Shield shown at left —led Hitler to believe that the Luftwaffe could sustain an entire army if it were cut off—a notion that within a year would be proved false at Stalingrad.

Those were sobering words, for Hitler's hopes of mastering destiny and dominating the East had been based on the assumption that the Wehrmacht would win a swift and devastating victory there as it had in the west. Instead, the Reich faced a long war of attrition for which it was ill prepared. The casualty tolls from the eastern front were appalling: Since June, more than a million German soldiers had been killed, wounded, or reported missing, and half a million more had been felled by illness or frostbite. The German armies in Russia were now short an estimated 625,000 men, and any simultaneous offensive by the three army groups was out of the question. That Hitler was haunted by the costly winter campaign became apparent a few days later, when he cut short a visit to the Berghof, his retreat in the Bavarian Alps. The reason? He explained tersely that he could no longer stand the sight of snow. ✚

"The Most Difficult Hour Has Begun"

Retreat was a stranger to this generation of German soldiers. But now Winter, a foe without mercy, lashed the battleground, and the unprotected Germans, with or without Hitler's blessing, turned back. The result was chaos and carnage. "The panzers' most difficult hour has begun," wrote a senior commander. Wheeled traffic clogged the few open roads. Combat troops who had fought since June without a rest retraced hard-won ground in somber columns *(right)* or in aimless clusters. They suffered greatly: Icy snow welded goggles to faces and bonded naked fingers to metal triggers. Soup froze before a soldier could spoon it to his mouth, and it took an ax to slice bread. Once a man fell, he was done for.

Hitler insisted that his troops "dig their nails into the ground." The order seemed insane, and he relieved thirty-five generals for questioning it. But his mulish determination to hold on had some merit. The stinging arctic winds and deep snow hampered the Soviet forces, too, even though they were better prepared. Unlike Napoléon Bonaparte's historic retreat to Paris, the German withdrawal was far from the homeward trek of a defeated army. The Wehrmacht pulled back only to defensible lines inside Russia, in some places within 100 miles of Moscow. There the German legions waited, their reputation tattered but their cadres largely intact, poised to strike again when spring finally came.

In a blizzard, German infantrymen stumble along the frozen ruts

of a road leading away from Moscow on December 6, 1941—two days before Hitler officially called off the assault on the capital.

Three Germans lie dead, shot as they fled a ruined farmhouse with plundered goods—including a samovar that the soldier at left

Above, German enlisted men
raise their hands in surrender,
becoming part of the 1,118,000
Germans who were killed,
wounded, or captured before
the winter came to an end.

Captured Germans huddle in
exhaustion under a shared
blanket. Such prisoners were
sent to labor camps in the Urals,
where most of them died of star-
vation, exposure, and overwork.

The road to Staraya Russa, a German supply depot and strongpoint south of the city of Leningrad, leads past graves that the Germans

had dug before the ground froze. The corpses at right must wait for burial until after the spring thaw.

Acknowledgments

The editors thank: England: London—Sophie Collins, John Calmann & King, Ltd.; Brian Davis; Christopher Hunt, Paul Kemp, Mike Willis, Imperial War Museum; Alexandra Wiessler, Wiener Library. Wareham Dorset—David Fletcher, George Forty, Tank Museum. Federal Republic of Germany: Berlin—Heidi Klein, Bildarchiv Preussischer Kulturbesitz; Gabrielle Kohler, Archiv für Kunst und Geschichte; Wolfgang Streubel, Ullstein Bilderdienst. Freiburg—Karl Diefenback, Militärgeschichtliches Forschungsamt. Hamburg—Paul Schmidt-Carell. Koblenz—Meinrad Nilges, Bundesarchiv. Munich—Elisabeth Heidt, Süddeutscher Verlag Bilderdienst. Oldenburg—Dieter Schmidt, Universitätsbibliothek. Rösrath-Hoffnungsthal—Helga Müller, Archiv Piekalkiewicz. France: Paris—Marie Vorobieff, Editions Larousse. United States of America: District of Columbia—Elizabeth Hill, Jim Trimble, National Archives; Eveline Nave, Library of Congress; George Snowden, Snowden Associates. North Carolina: Wolfgang O. Horn. New Jersey—Al Collett. Virginia—George A. Petersen, National Capital Historical Sales.

Picture Credits

Credits from left to right are separated by semicolons, from top to bottom by dashes. Cover: From *Signal* magazine, February 1, 1942, courtesy George A. Petersen. 4, 5: From *Signal* magazine, September 2, 1941, courtesy George A. Petersen. 6, 7: Bildarchiv Preussischer Kulturbesitz, West Berlin. 8, 9: Archiv Gerstenberg, Wietze. 10, 11: Archiv für Kunst und Geschichte, West Berlin. 12, 13: Military Archives and Research Services, Brace Borough, Lincolnshire. 14, 15: Archiv für Kunst und Geschichte, West Berlin. 16: Bundesarchiv, Koblenz. 19: Universitäts-bibliothek, Oldenburg. 20, 21: U.S. Naval Institute, Annapolis. 23: Süddeutscher Verlag Bilderdienst, Munich. 24, 25: Sovfoto/Eastfoto; Brian Davis Collection, London. 27: Map by R. R. Donnelley and Sons Company, Cartographic Services. 30: Bundesarchiv, Koblenz. 31-33: Ullstein Bilderdienst, West Berlin. 34, 35: Art by John Batchelor. 36: Ullstein Bilderdienst, West Berlin. 37: The Tank Museum, Bovington Camp, Dorset. 38, 39: From *Die Guten Glaubens Waren*, Munin-Verlag, Osnabruck. 41: Courtesy Time Inc. Magazines Picture Collection. 42, 43: Bildarchiv Preussischer Kulturbesitz, West Berlin. 45: Bundesarchiv, Koblenz. 46, 47: Süddeutscher Verlag Bilderdienst, Munich—Bundesarchiv, Koblenz; National Archives no. 242-GAP-235-D-16—from *Unternehmen Barbarossa im Bild: Der Russlandkrieg Fotografiert von Soldaten* by Paul Carell, Ullstein Verlag, Frankfurt, 1967. 48, 49: Bundesarchiv, Koblenz; Ullstein Bilderdienst, West Berlin. 51: Map by R. R. Donnelley and Sons Company, Cartographic Services. 52, 53: Ullstein Bilderdienst, West Berlin; Süddeutscher Verlag Bilderdienst, Munich. 54, 55: Ullstein Bilderdienst, West Berlin. 56: Photo Archives, Larousse. 58, 59: Photograph by Margaret Bourke-White for LIFE; Camera Press, London. 61: Map by R. R. Donnelley and Sons Company, Cartographic Services. 62-64: Bildarchiv Preussischer Kulturbesitz, West Berlin. 65: Map by R. R. Donnelley and Sons Company, Cartographic Services. 66, 67: Ullstein Bilderdienst, West Berlin. 68, 69: Bundesarchiv, Koblenz. 70, 71: UPI/Bettmann Newsphotos. 73: Map by R. R. Donnelley and Sons Company, Cartographic Services. 74, 75: Ullstein Bilderdienst, West Berlin; Süddeutscher Verlag Bilderdienst, Munich. 77: Ullstein Bilderdienst, West Berlin. 79-81: Larry Sherer, courtesy George A. Petersen and Roger Hall. 82, 83: Bundesarchiv, Koblenz. 84: Sovfoto/Eastfoto. 85: Map by R. R. Donnelley and Sons Company, Cartographic Services. 86, 87: Süddeutscher Verlag Bilderdienst, Munich; Ullstein Bilderdienst, West Berlin. 89: Archives Tallandier, Paris. 90, 91: Photograph by Nikolai Khandogin. 92, 93: Novosti, Moscow, except upper right Nikolai Khandogin. 94: Private collection. 95: Camera Press, London. 96, 97: Sovfoto/Eastfoto—Novosti, Moscow; Sovfoto/Eastfoto. 98: Private collection. 99-101: Photograph by Boris Kudoyarov. 102: Bildarchiv Preussischer Kulturbesitz, West Berlin, foto A. Grimm. 105: Map by R. R. Donnelley and Sons Company, Cartographic Services. 106, 107: Photograph by Alexander Ustinov. 109-111: Bundesarchiv, Koblenz. 112, 113: From the collection of Stephen Flood; Ullstein Bilderdienst, West Berlin. 114, 115: Bundesarchiv, Koblenz, except center Süddeutscher Verlag Bilderdienst, Munich. 116: Novosti, Moscow. 117: Sovfoto/Eastfoto. 118, 119: Map by R. R. Donnelley and Sons Company, Cartographic Services—from *Unternehmen Barbarossa im Bild: Der Russlandkrieg Fotografiert von Soldaten* by Paul Carell, Ullstein Verlag, Frankfurt, 1967. 120, 121: Map by R. R. Donnelley and Sons Company, Cartographic Services; courtesy Alex Buchner, Dillishausen. 122, 123: Bundesarchiv, Koblenz. 125: Ullstein Bilderdienst, West Berlin. 127: AP/Wide World Photos. 128: Ullstein Bilderdienst, West Berlin. 129: Map by R. R. Donnelley and Sons Company, Cartographic Services. 130, 131: National Archives no. 242-GAP-238I-14. 132, 133: Bildarchiv Preussischer Kulturbesitz, West Berlin. 135: Courtesy Dr. Wolfgang O. Horn—Steve Tuttle, courtesy Dr. Wolfgang O. Horn. 136-145: Courtesy Dr. Wolfgang O. Horn, compass on page 139 photographed by Larry Sherer. 146: Hulton Deutsch Picture Collection, London. 149: Sovfoto/Eastfoto. 151: Map by R. R. Donnelley and Sons Company, Cartographic Services. 152, 153: UPI/Bettmann Newsphotos. 155: Camera Press, London. 156, 157: Ullstein Bilderdienst, West Berlin. 158, 159: Photo A.P.N. 163: Map by R. R. Donnelley and Sons Company, Cartographic Services. 165: UPI/Bettmann Newsphotos. 166: Larry Sherer, courtesy Kirk Denkler. 169: Photographed by Larry Sherer, from *Kampfgruppe Scherer* by Richard Muck, Gerhard Stalling Verlag, 1943—Bundesarchiv, Koblenz. 170, 171: Bundesarchiv, Koblenz, except bottom left from *Kampfgruppe Scherer* by Richard Muck, Gerhard Stalling Verlag, Oldenburg, 1943. 172: Ullstein Bilderdienst, West Berlin; Larry Sherer, courtesy Kirk Denkler. 175: Map by R. R. Donnelley and Sons Company, Cartographic Services. 176, 177: Bundesarchiv, Koblenz—Larry Sherer, courtesy George A. Petersen. 178, 179: Archiv Piekalkiewicz: Rösrath-Hoffnungsthal. 180-182: Sovfoto/Eastfoto. 183: Photo A.P.N. 184, 185: From *The Great Patriotic War*, 1942, Planeta, Moscow, 1986.

Bibliography

Adamovich, Ales, and Daniil Granin, *A Book of the Blockade*. Moscow: Raduga, 1983.

Angolia, John R., and Adolf Schlicht, *Uniforms and Traditions of the German Army, 1933-1945*. Vols. 1 and 3. San Jose, Calif.: R. James Bender, 1984, 1987.

Bekker, Cajus, *The Luftwaffe War Diaries*. Ed. and transl. by Frank Ziegler. Garden City, N.Y.: Doubleday, 1968.

Boog, Horst, et al., *Der Angriff auf die Sowjetunion*. Vol. 4 of *Das Deutsche Reich und der Zweite Weltkrieg*. Stuttgart, W.Ger.: Deutsche Verlags-Anstalt, 1983.

Brett-Smith, Richard, *Hitler's Generals*. San Rafael, Calif.: Presidio Press, 1977.

Buchner, Alex, *Vom Eismeer bis zum Kaukasus: Die Deutsche Gebirgstruppe im Zweiten Weltkrieg, 1941/42*. Friedberg, W.Ger.: Podzun-Pallas-Verlag, 1988.

Burdick, Charles, and Hans-Adolf Jacobsen, eds., *The Halder War Diary, 1939-1942*. Novato, Calif.: Presidio Press, 1988.

Carell, Paul:
Hitler Moves East, 1941-1943. Transl. by Ewald Osers. Boston: Little, Brown, 1964.
Der Russlandkrieg: Fotografiert von Soldaten. Berlin: Ullstein, 1967.

Clark, Alan, *Barbarossa: The Russian-German Conflict, 1941-45*. New York: William Morrow, 1965.

Culver, Bruce:
PzKpfw III in Action. Carrollton, Tex.: Squadron/Signal, 1988.
Sturmgeschütz III in Action. Carrollton, Tex.: Squadron/Signal, 1976.

Dallin, Alexander, *German Rule in Russia, 1941-1945: A Study of Occupation Policies*. Boulder, Colo.: Westview Press, 1981.

Erickson, John, *The Road to Stalingrad: Stalin's War with Germany*. Boulder, Colo.: Westview Press, 1984.

Fugate, Bryan I., *Operation Barbarossa: Strategy and Tactics on the Eastern Front, 1941*. Novato, Calif.: Presidio Press, 1984.

Guderian, Heinz, *Panzer Leader*. Transl. by Constantine FitzGibbon. New York: E. P. Dutton, 1952.

Hilberg, Raul, *The Destruction of the European Jews*. New York: Holmes & Meier, 1985.

Huber, Heinz, and Artur Müller, eds., *Der Zusammenbruch der Macht*. Vol. 2 of *Das Dritte Reich*. Munich: Verlag Kurt Desch, 1964.

Irving, David, *Hitler's War*. London: Hodder and Stoughton, 1977.

Karpov, Vladimir, *Russia at War, 1941-45*. Transl. by Lydia Kmetyuk. New York: Vendome Press, 1987.

Kreipe, Werner, et al., *The Fatal Decisions*. Transl. by Constantine FitzGibbon. New York: Berkley, 1958.

Littlejohn, David, and C. M. Dodkins, *Orders, Decorations, Medals and Badges of the Third Reich*. Mountain View, Calif.: R. James Bender, 1970.

Lucas, James:
Alpine Elite: German Mountain Troops of World War II. London: Jane's, 1980.
War on the Eastern Front, 1941-1945: The German Soldier in Russia. London: Jane's, 1979.

Macksey, Kenneth, *Guderian: Creator of the Blitzkrieg*. New York: Stein and Day, 1976.

Malaparte, Curzio, *The Volga Rises in Europe*. Transl. by David Moore. London: Alvin Redman, 1957.

Manstein, Erich von, *Lost Victories*. Ed. and transl. by Anthony G. Powell. Chicago: Henry Regnery, 1958.

Muck, Richard, *Kampfgruppe Scherer: 105 Tage Eingeschlossen*. Berlin: Gerhard Stalling Verlag, 1943.

Paget, R. T., *Manstein: His Campaigns and His Trial*. London: Collins, 1951.

Perrett, Bryan, *Knights of the Black Cross: Hitler's Panzerwaffe and Its Leaders*. New York: St. Martin's Press, 1986.

Piekalkiewicz, Janusz, *Moscow, 1941: The Frozen Offensive*. Novato, Calif.: Presidio Press, 1981.

Salisbury, Harrison E.:
The 900 Days: The Siege of Leningrad. New York: Harper & Row, 1969.
The Unknown War. New York: Bantam Books, 1978.

Seaton, Albert, *The Russo-German War, 1941-45*. New York: Praeger, 1972.

Senger und Etterlin, F. M. von, *German Tanks of World War II*. Transl. by J. Lucas. New York: Galahad Books, 1969.

Stoves, Rolf, *Die Gepanzerten und Motorisierten Deutschen Grossverbände (Divisionen und Selbständige Brigaden), 1935-1945*. Friedberg, W.Ger.: Podzun-Pallas-Verlag, 1986.

Toland, John, *Adolf Hitler*. Vol. 2. Garden City, N.Y.: Doubleday, 1976.

Trevor-Roper, H. R., ed., *Blitzkrieg to Defeat: Hitler's War Directives, 1939-1945*. New York: Holt, Rinehart and Winston, 1965.

Turney, Alfred W., *Disaster at Moscow: Von Bock's Campaigns, 1941-1942*. Albuquerque: University of New Mexico Press, 1970.

Van Creveld, Martin L., *Hitler's Strategy, 1940-1941: The Balkan Clue*. London: Cambridge University Press, 1973.

Werth, Alexander, *Russia at War, 1941-1945*. New York: Carroll & Graf, 1986.

Wykes, Alan, *The Siege of Leningrad: Epic of Survival*. New York: Ballantine Books, 1972.

Zaloga, Steven J., and James Grandsen, *Operation Barbarossa*. Vol. 16 of *Tanks Illustrated*. London: Arms and Armour Press, 1985.

Ziemke, Earl F., and Magna E. Bauer, *Moscow to Stalingrad: Decision in the East*. Washington, D.C.: Center of Military History, United States Army, 1987.

Index